In the Footsteps of Jesus and the Apostles

Published by Eagle Publishing Ltd, 6 Kestrel House, Mill Street, Trowbridge, Wiltshire BA14 8BE.

British Library Cataloguing in Publication Data. A catalogue record for this book is available from the British Library.

Typeset by Eagle Publishing Ltd
Printed in China
ISBN No. 0 86347 583 3

In the Footsteps of Jesus and the Apostles

Text by Stephen Sizer

Photographs by Jon Arnold

eagle

Bath, England

Contents

A VIEW OF EGIRDIR LAKE, PISIDIAN ANTIOCH

Preface

MASADA, NEAR DEAD SEA, JORDAN RIFT VALLEY, ISRAEL

A book like this is precious both for what it can give and because it whets our appetites for more: if you have seen the country then it will revive your memories and recollections; if you have not, it may inspire you with eagerness to do so.

This is a book to savour. Each page introduces you to another place steeped in biblical history and abiding relevance. This is indeed the birthplace of our faith in the Lord Jesus Christ.

But there is much more to see in the Holy Land than ancient archaeological sites. There is here a vibrant but ancient church that has been here witnessing faithfully to Christ since the first Pentecost. If and when you do come, make it a priority to meet with us, the local Christians of your mother Church. Take time to visit a school or hospital run by one of the churches in Israel and Palestine. Our very future here is at stake.

May I extend to you a heartfelt welcome on behalf of your brothers and sisters in Christ – come and visit the land these moving photographs portray, and have fellowship with us. Then we shall both be enriched and blessed.

I pray that this book will enrich your sympathies and deepen your knowledge of the events which have made Palestine a Holy Land and Jerusalem the joy of the whole earth, a synonym of the City of God.

Riah Abu El-Assal, Anglican Bishop of Jerusalem

Foreword

After the success of Stephen Sizer's first book, *A Panorama of the Holy Land,* this sequel (which reaches further into the Mediterranean and Middle East) is sure to attract a wide readership. *In the Footsteps of Jesus and the Apostles* might well have borrowed the title of a well – known 19th – century volume by George Adam Smith entitled *The Historical Geography of the Holy Land.* For it is a fine blend of history, geography, biblical allusion and Christian teaching.

Like the ripples caused by a bird landing on water, we are taken on a journey outward from Palestine, following the Apostles as they are commissioned by the risen Christ and empowered by the Holy Spirit to be his witnesses in the major cities of the Roman empire including Ephesus, Pergamum, Colosse, Corinth, Athens and Rome.

The text itself is long enough to be satisfying and yet brief enough to be accessible to the reader. Its contemporary applications are

6

always relevant and often challenging. It has always been a salutary exercise for the Christian Church in each generation to compare itself with the early Church. Stephen not only draws out the relevant historical and biblical significance of each site, but seeks to highlight its contemporary relevance also. We are reminded, as the New Testament proclaims, that we believe in both the historical Jesus who lived and the contemporary Jesus who lives.

Bible students will enjoy looking up its many references. Would-be pilgrims will use it to prepare for their visit. Those who have already been will be helped to re-live their experience. And those who will never have the chance to go will be able, through the descriptive text and stunning pictures, to imagine the scenes whose names are so familiar. Particularly striking are the 30 or so double-page full colour spreads which occur every few pages and give us spectacular panoramic views.

Luke ends the Acts of the Apostles confidently with Paul preaching, *'boldly and without hindrance'* symbolising the wide open door for the gospel (Acts 28:31). In that sense it is an unfinished book. Although some of the places described here are no longer known for their living Christian presence owing to persecution, it is our privilege to step into their shoes and to make Christ known in our generation. May this book remind you of our heritage and inspire you to fulfil our high calling.

John Stott

JUDEAN DESERT APPROACHING JERICHO

A VIEW OF
THE PROMISED
LAND FROM
MOUNT NEBO

'Palestine', 'Israel', the 'Promised Land' – the very name we use says as much about us and our presuppositions as about this inscrutable, hypnotic, exotic location.

Historically the birthplace of the Judeo-Christian heritage, it is today claimed by two peoples, the Jews and Palestinians, its holy sites shared, at times uneasily, by three religions, Jewish, Christian and Moslem, often in close proximity as at the Temple Mount in Jerusalem or the tomb of Rachel in Bethlehem.

Barbara Tuchman summarises some of the reasons why this place holds such fascination to so many, '*More blood has been shed for Palestine than for any other spot on earth. To Protestant England it was not only, as Lord Curzon said, "the holiest space of ground on the face of the globe," the land of the Scriptures, the land of the Crusades, the land "to which all our faces are turned when we are finally laid in our graves in the churchyard." It was also the geographical junction between East and West, the bridge-head between three continents, the focal point in the strategy of empire.'*

Few countries attract as much media coverage, arouse such intense religious emotion or political controversy. Yet it has done so for countless generations. Why have people for millennia longed to conquer, live here, or make a pilgrimage to this land? What is the fascination this land has over so many people around the world?

The Holy Land has been described as '*the fifth gospel*'. This book aspires to give you a glimpse into the world of that fifth gospel. Through brief notes and stunning pictures it is designed to inform your mind, stir your heart and deepen your faith. This unique book provides an introduction to the history, geography and biblical significance of over 30 of the most important places that feature in the Bible.

Local Christians like to call it 'the Land of the Holy One' for it is here that God has come to dwell with us and make himself known uniquely in the person of Jesus Christ. It was here that heaven and earth, time and eternity met in Jesus Christ. Many testify to having encountered him in a deeper way at one or more of these locations. Whether you have visited the Holy Land many times before or may be contemplating doing so, may this book enhance your faith.

Christianity is first and foremost an historical faith. It is not primarily a philosophy or an ethical code but is based on the space – time intervention by God in human history in the person of Jesus Christ. In this book you are introduced to the most important geographical locations associated with Jesus, from his birth in Bethlehem, through his ministry in Galilee, to his death and resurrection in Jerusalem.

Christianity is also a missionary faith. After his resurrection Jesus Christ sent out his apostles to go into all the world and make disciples, teaching them to obey all he had commanded them. This book takes you on that journey of faith tracing the steps of Paul and the other disciples recorded in the Acts of the Apostles. We witness how the first disciples systematically shared the good news of

SOLOMON'S PILLARS, TIMNA PARK

Jesus Christ in each major town and city of the Roman Empire until they finally reached the capital of Rome itself.

Above all, Christianity is a living faith. Whether you are already a Christian or not, reflect on each location and read the biblical references offered to dig deeper into the Scriptures. See how God has used each place within his providential purposes to reveal his love for you. My prayer is that *In the Footsteps of Jesus and the Apostles* you may develop a deeper love for the Holy One who was predicted, born, lived, died and rose here, that you might live for ever. But don't let that good news stop with you, pass it on!

Stephen R. Sizer

DONKEY, MOUNT OF OLIVES

SUNRISE, SEA OF GALILEE

Mount Sinai

When Moses went up on the mountain, the cloud covered it, and the glory of the LORD settled on Mount Sinai. For six days the cloud covered the mountain, and on the seventh day the LORD called to Moses from within the cloud. To the Israelites the glory of the LORD looked like a consuming fire on top of the mountain. Then Moses entered the cloud as he went on up the mountain. And he stayed on the mountain forty days and forty nights. (Exodus 24:15–18)

Mount Sinai which is also called Mount Horeb, lies within the Sinai Peninsula, a large wedge-shaped land bridge between Africa and Asia bounded by the Gulf of Suez, the Mediterranean, the Gulf of Aqaba and the Red Sea. The exact location of Mount Sinai is not known but it is believed to be near Ras Sasafeh where the mountain range climbs almost vertically from the Sinai Plain. Dean Stanley, the nineteenth-century explorer describes how the dramatic scenery, '….presents a long retiring sweep, within which the people could remove and stand afar off. The cliff, rising like a huge altar in front of the whole congregation, and visible against the sky in lonely grandeur from end to end of the whole plain, is the very image of the "mount that might be touched", and from which the voice of God might be heard far and wide over the plain below.'

Having left Egypt a few months before, the people of Israel journeyed about 240 kilometres and camped in 'the Desert of Sinai' at the foot of the mountain. There they stayed for a whole year (Exodus 19:1–2; Numbers 10:11–13). It was there on Mount Sinai that the Lord God revealed himself through Moses to Israel (Exodus 19:17–24). The Law of God was given (Exodus 20), the role of the Levite priests established (Numbers 3), the first tabernacle built (Numbers 9:15), and the covenant between God and Israel confirmed (Exodus 24). So significant was this event that the mountain came to symbolise God's awesome presence and protection (Judges 5:4–5; Psalm 68:7–8). The other events that occurred when Israel camped at the foot of Mount Sinai are recorded in Exodus 19–40, Leviticus and Numbers 1–11.

Following his victory over the 450 prophets of Baal at Mount Carmel, Elijah, exhausted and afraid of Jezebel's threats of revenge, fled to Mount Sinai. Here the Lord graciously appeared to him, not in the wind or earthquake, but in the still small voice. Elijah was re-commissioned to anoint two new kings, and Elisha as his successor (1 Kings 19:1–18).

There are also a number of significant references and allusions to Mount Sinai in the New Testament. Like Moses, Jesus spent 40 days alone in the wilderness (Luke 4:1–13). In his transfiguration on another high mountain, Jesus encountered Moses and Elijah both of whom had met with God on Mount Sinai. The shekinah glory of God as well as the voice of God confirmed Christ's authority (Matthew 17:1–5). In another allusion to Mount Sinai, Jesus compares himself with the cursed snake lifted up by Moses to save those being punished for their rebellion (John 3:13-15). After Jesus had been rejected and crucified, Sinai came to be associated with those still in slavery under the old covenant. This is contrasted with those set free to be the true children of God by faith through the new covenant (Galatians 4:24–25; Hebrews 12:18–24). It was actually God, not Moses, who provided food and water for the Israelites in the wilderness (John 6:32). Paul even asserts that Christ was the very Rock (1 Corinthians 10:4). One greater than Moses has now appeared (Hebrews 3:2–6).

The experience of Israel in the wilderness of Sinai is used as a sober lesson to warn Christians not to commit the same sins of idolatry and unbelief which led to God's judgement (1 Corinthians 10:1–13; Hebrews 3:7–19). We must never become complacent or, worse still, arrogant about the basis of our salvation. The genuineness of our faith in Christ is evidenced not by our profession but by our perseverance.

MOUNT SINAI IS A SUCCESSION OF ARID PILLARS

Beersheba

'Abraham planted a tamarisk tree in Beersheba, and there he called upon the name of the LORD, the Eternal God. And Abraham stayed in the land of the Philistines for a long time.' (Genesis 21:33–34)

Beersheba is an ancient town marking the southern limit of Israeli settlement in biblical times on the northern edge of the Negev Desert. It lies on the trade route to Egypt, midway between Gaza and the Mediterranean Sea to the west and the Dead Sea to the east, about 77 kilometres from Jerusalem to the north. At Beersheba several important personal encounters with God took place. These include Hagar (Genesis 21:8–17); Isaac (Genesis 26:23–33); Jacob (Genesis 46:1–5); and Elijah (1 Kings 19:3).

At Beersheba God taught his people many lessons in how to relate to their neighbours, some of which are still relevant today. It was here that Hagar, the Egyptian servant of Sarah, and her son Ishmael, abandoned by Abraham in the desert, encountered the angel of God. God promised not only that they would survive but that Ishmael would become the father of a great nation (Genesis 21:14–21). This promise was fulfilled in the rise of the Arab peoples. It was also here in the land of the Philistines, living as an alien, that Abraham learnt to call on the name of the Lord. He dug a well and planted a tamarisk tree after agreeing a treaty with Abimelech, king of Gerar over rights to the water (Genesis 21:22–34).

The name Beersheba means 'the well of the seven' and refers to the seven lambs offered as witness to the covenant of mutual assistance between the Patriarch and the Philistines (Genesis 21:31). Beersheba appears to have been the home of Abraham and Isaac, for when the dispute arose between Jacob and Esau over the birthright, it was from Beersheba that Jacob began his journey to Mesopotamia

WELL SHAFT

TAMARISK TREES IN AN OASIS NEAR BEERSHEBA

in search of a wife (Genesis 28:10). Many years later Jacob, now called Israel, offered sacrifices to God at Beersheba on his way to Egypt to be reunited with his son Joseph (Genesis 46:1). In the times of the Judges, the people of Israel cried out for a king, because of the corrupt leadership of Samuel's sons Joel and Abijah at Beersheba (1 Samuel 8:2). When Jezebel tried to kill Elijah he fled to Beersheba and, like Hagar, prayed that he might die there. Here in the desert the Lord sustained Elijah and commissioned him to anoint a new generation of religious and political leaders (1 Kings 19:1–9).

The kingdom in David's time stretched from 'Dan to Beersheba' and this expression came to denote the extent of Israeli settlement from north to south (2 Samuel 17:11). Perhaps because of the associations with the Patriarchs and with the theophanies which occurred there, by the time of Amos, Beersheba had become one of the idolatrous shrines rivalling the true worship of God in Jerusalem. Amos' message remains pertinent when we too are tempted, 'Seek the Lord and live' (Amos 5:4–6; 8:14).

Beersheba reminds us that it is often in our desert experiences, when we are brought low and realise we cannot rely on human resources, that we encounter God afresh. We discover like the Patriarchs did that as we worship him as the one true God of heaven and earth and trust in him alone, he will not only sustain us but give us new direction and purpose.

DESERT LANDSCAPE NEAR BEERSHEBA

The Judean Wilderness

'I will make rivers flow on barren heights, and springs within the valleys. I will turn the desert into pools of water, and the parched ground into springs. I will put in the desert the cedar and the acacia, the myrtle and the olive ... so that people may see and know, may consider and understand, that the hand of the LORD has done this, that the Holy One of Israel has created it'. (Isaiah 41:18–20)

The Judean wilderness roughly extends from the shores of the Dead Sea, west through the mountainous central plateau before it begins to descend to the coastal plains near Gaza by the Mediterranean Sea (Judges 1:16). To the south lies the more inhospitable wilderness of Sinai (Exodus 19:1) and to the north, Jerusalem and the hills of Samaria. The word Judea is the Greco-Latin form of Judah. The term Judah was used by Ezra to describe the area of Palestine around Jerusalem which was then under Persian rule (Ezra 5:8). There are only three natural springs on the eastern edge of the Judean wilderness, at Jericho, Ain Feshka, 16 kilometres to the south, and at En Gedi another 28 kilometres further south.

The word used to describe this wilderness in Hebrew is *midbar*, meaning 'pasture-ground' and denotes land without settled inhabitants or natural sources of water. The word is also used to describe the wilderness between Egypt and Palestine where the tribes of Israel wandered with their flocks and herds for 40 years (Exodus 19:2; Jeremiah 2:6). This area is known as a 'tame desert' because of its latent fertility needing only water to make it fruitful. It receives limited rainfall of between 100-300 millimetres a year, although amounts can vary dramatically from

JUDEAN DESERT NEAR WADI QELT (NAHAL PERAT)

WADI QELT (NAHAL PERAT)

year to year. The wilderness of Judea is prone to sudden storms causing dangerous flash floods which tend to occur in March or April. The erosion caused by these floods leave a dramatic mark on the landscape. For a matter of only a few weeks, when rain has fallen, the Judean wilderness is carpeted in a brief but beautiful display of flowers and greenery (Isaiah 35:1–2).

The Bible depicts the desert as the habitat of raiders such as the Amalekites and Midianites who frequently attacked the Israelite farmers. They were sent by God to punish the Jews for rebelling against him (Judges 6:1–6). Saul was eventually able to provide some measure of relief from these attacks (1 Samuel 14:47–48). It was here that David shepherded his father's flocks (1 Samuel 17:28; 26:1–3) and found refuge from Saul (1 Samuel 23:21–29). Two of the prophets were born here, Amos at Tekoa and Jeremiah at Anathoth. John the Baptist also lived and preached in the Judean wilderness (Luke 1:80; 3:1–6).

The inhospitable desert was held in fear and awe by the Jews, a place of terror (Isaiah 21:1). The Israelites were warned to remember how the Lord protected them from its harsh climate and 'venomous snakes and scorpions' when later they were tempted to become proud and arrogant (Deuteronomy 8:10–20). Figuratively, the desert was also used to depict the graphic effects of God's judgement (Isaiah 33:8–9), returning the earth to its primeval chaos as it was before creation (Jeremiah 4:23–26).

NAHAL PERAT, JUDEAN DESERT

The Dead Sea

He said to me, 'This water flows towards the eastern region and goes down into the Arabah, where it enters the Sea. When it empties into the Sea, the water there becomes fresh. Swarms of living creatures will live wherever the river flows. There will be large numbers of fish, because this water flows there and makes the salt water fresh; so where the river flows everything will live'. (Ezekiel 47:8–9)

The Dead Sea marks the lowest point on earth and formed Israel's eastern border. In the Bible it is called by various names including the Salt Sea (Genesis 14:3); the Sea of the Arabah (Joshua 3:16); and the Eastern Sea (Ezekiel 47:18). The Middle East is dominated by a geological fault line which runs from Syria down to Central Africa. The Dead Sea is at the southern end of the Jordan Valley which has been shaped by this fault line. The water level is around 390 metres or

A PALM TREE ON THE NORTHERN EDGE OF THE DEAD SEA

1,300 feet below sea level. The size of the Dead Sea has changed a great deal in history. Today it is approximately 80 kilometres from north to south and 15 kilometres from east to west. In recent years it has been shrinking due to the removal of water from the Jordan River for irrigation. Because there is no outlet for the water, evaporation leaves behind large quantities of mineral deposits such as potash, bromine, magnesium chloride, and other salts, making the Dead Sea, at around 30 per cent solid, the source of the richest mineral deposits on earth. The region also suffers from an inhospitable climate reaching 43°C in summer with an average rainfall of only 5 cm per year.

The shores of the Dead Sea feature in many biblical events. It is believed that the cities of Sodom and Gomorrah were situated near its southern shores (Genesis 13:10–12; 19:24). On its western side the freshwater spring of En Gedi provided a place of refuge for David, when hiding from Saul (1 Samuel 24:1–2); to the south, in the Valley of Salt, David was victorious over the Edomites (1 Chronicles 18:12-13) as was Jehoshaphat at the Pass of Ziz just north of En Gedi (2 Chronicles

20:1–3, 15–17). Herod the Great built one of his fortresses at Machaerus in Perea overlooking the eastern shores of the Dead Sea. It was here that John the Baptist was later imprisoned and beheaded by Herod Antipas (Mark 6:14–29).

Although the Dead Sea is associated, as its name suggests, with death and barrenness, the prophet Ezekiel saw a wonderful vision of a river flowing out from the temple sanctuary in Jerusalem and down through the Judean wilderness into the Dead Sea (Ezekiel 47:1–12). The prophet Zechariah also prophesied, 'On that day living water will flow out from Jerusalem, half to the eastern sea and half to the western sea, in summer and in winter' (Zechariah 14:8). The apostle John refers to the same glorious hope in his vision of Revelation 22. Jesus gave new meaning, to the phrase 'living water' in his conversation with the woman at the well of Samaria in John 4 and later in his teaching, in the temple itself in John 7.

'On the last and greatest day of the Feast, Jesus stood and said in a loud voice, "If anyone is thirsty, let him come to me and drink. Whoever believes in me, as the Scripture has said, streams of living water will flow from within him"' (John 7:37–38).

There are times perhaps when we can identify with the psalmist David who cried out when he was in the Judean wilderness near the Dead Sea, 'O God, you are my God, earnestly I seek you; my soul thirsts for you, my body longs for you, in a dry and weary land where there is no water' (Psalm 63:1). The good news is we don't have to visit the shores of the Dead Sea to develop a thirst for the Holy Spirit, whom Jesus promised to all who seek him.

A FIERCE SUN BEATS DOWN RELENTLESSLY ON THE DEAD SEA

DEAD SEA JORDAN RIFT VALLEY
(OVERLEAF)

En Gedi

My lover is to me a cluster of henna blossoms from the vineyards of En Gedi. (Song of Songs 1:14)

Along the western shore of the Dead Sea, the barren hills of the Judean wilderness descend through deep ridges and, for most of the year, dry gullies. Freshwater springs are rare but the most spectacular and abundant is to be found about midway along the shore at En Gedi, some 30 kilometres south-east of Hebron.

Hot water springs burst from the ground about 100 metres above the cliff base forming a beautiful cascading waterfall sustaining a semi-tropical oasis of rich vegetation.

NAHAL ARUGOT WATERFALL, EN GEDI

DATE PALMS FRINGE THE OASIS OF EN GEDI

Aptly named, En Gedi means 'spring' or 'fountain of the kid'. It was first known as Hazezon Tamar which means 'pruning of palms' suggesting that date palms also once grew here (Genesis 14:7; 2 Chronicles 20:2). En Gedi was inhabited by the Amorites in the days of Abraham (Genesis 14:7), was allotted to Judah (Joshua 15:62), and in the reign of Solomon was renowned for its vineyards (Song 1:14). It was also an important source of aromatic and medicinal plants including henna and balsam. Archaeological remains dated to the time of Josiah (c. 639–609 BC) show evidence that perfumes were produced here.

En Gedi is probably remembered most of all for being the place of refuge where David hid from King Saul and his army of 3,000 men (1 Samuel 23:29–24:1). There are many caves in the area of En Gedi and on one occasion the rugged terrain enabled David to take advantage of Saul who had entered a cave to relieve himself. David's men took this as a providential sign that they should kill Saul (1 Samuel 24:4). This would have secured David's claim to the throne, already confirmed by Samuel (1 Samuel 16:13). David, however, resisted the temptation. In his conscience he knew that such an action was wrong. It was not cowardice but courage David displayed in refusing to kill Saul. He acknowledged that God had appointed Saul and God alone would judge between them, vindicating David at the right time (1 Samuel 24:12–15; 26:10–11).

It was an important lesson David learnt about patience and trusting in the revealed character of God. Perhaps David shared this experience with his son Solomon for he later wrote, 'The king's heart is in the hand of the LORD; he directs it like a watercourse wherever he pleases' (Proverbs 21:1).

The events of David's experience in En Gedi remind us not to interpret our own circumstances too quickly or necessarily read into them God's providence, even when the advice of others coincides. The ends rarely justify the means. Instead we should weigh our circumstances carefully in the light of our conscience and above all in the light of God's Word. We should not compromise our moral standards by giving in to group pressure or by taking the easy way out. David used those times alone with God to meditate on God's character and promises. The best way to develop a similar intimacy with God is to take time alone with him and with an open Bible find nourishment and refreshment at your very own spiritual En Gedi. The Psalms, many of which were inspired in this region, are a good place to start (see Psalms 18;54; 56–57; 59; 63; 142).

WATERFALL AT EN GEDI

Megiddo and the Jezreel Valley

THE NORTH GATE, MEGIDDO

And I will pour out on the house of David and the inhabitants of Jerusalem a spirit of grace and supplication. They will look on me, the one they have pierced, and they will mourn for him as one mourns for an only child, and grieve bitterly for him as one grieves for a firstborn son. On that day the weeping in Jerusalem will be great, like the weeping of Hadad Rimmon in the plain of Megiddo. (Zechariah 12:10–11)

Megiddo is the most strategic location in Palestine and possibly in the entire Middle East. Situated at the entrance to the main pass through the Carmel mountains, it lies on the junction of two important historic roads used by armies and traders from the Stone Age to the present day. Megiddo guards access to the Mediterranean Sea in the west and the route east through the Jezreel Valley to Damascus and Mesopotamia. The other coastal route links Egypt and Gaza in the south with Acco and Phoenicia in the north.

Control of Megiddo, therefore, has been of military importance since at least the days of Thutmose III in the fifteenth century BC right up to General Allenby's campaigns in the First World War. Jezreel, which means 'God sows' (in Greek, *Esdraelon*), separates the hills of Samaria from those of Lower Galilee. It is so flat it is possible to

see for fifty kilometres in several directions. It is easy to imagine how great armies once camped within it on twenty different occasions.

The imposing Tell at Megiddo stands 21 metres high and archaeology has revealed over twenty distinct periods of occupation.

THE WATER TUNNEL AT MEGIDDO

30

Megiddo was once one of the royal fortified cities of the Canaanites (Joshua 12:21) and before that it was of importance within the Egyptian empire. It was assigned by God to the tribe of Manasseh (Judges 1:27) but was not captured until the time of Solomon when it became one of his administrative districts (Joshua 17:11–13;1 Kings 4:12; 9:15). During the period of the Judges the Israelites rebelled against God. He allowed Jabin the Canaanite king to oppress them for twenty years. When they cried out to God, he sent Deborah the prophetess to lead Israel (Judges 4:1–14). She inspired Barak and the northern tribes to gather near Mount Tabor to ambush Sisera and his 900 chariots. The Canaanites were defeated and Sisera came to a messy end in the tent of Jael (Judges 4:15–24).

Megiddo became one of Solomon's principal fortified cities like those at Hazor and Gezer. Extensive stables have been discovered large enough to accommodate 450 horses. These possibly date from the time of Solomon or more probably belonged to Ahab. During the divided monarchy, Megiddo again fell into the hands of the Egyptians and then to the Assyrians. In 609 BC Pharaoh Neco II and his Egyptian army passed through the Valley of Jezreel on his way to fight against the Assyrians. King Josiah ignored God's guidance and tried to resist the Egyptians at Megiddo but was fatally wounded by an Egyptian archer and died in battle there (2 Kings 23:29; 2 Chronicles 35:20–24). The prophet Zechariah, speaking prophetically, compared the mourning of King Josiah in Jerusalem with that of the crucified Lord (Zechariah 12:10–12). Summarising the importance of the Valley of Jezreel in biblical history, George Adam Smith writes, 'Esdraelon lies before you . . . the scenes of Barak's and Gideon's victories, of Saul's and Josiah's defeats, of the struggles for freedom in the glorious days of the Maccabees. There is Naboth's vineyard and the place of Jehu's revenge upon Jezebel; there Shunem and the house of Elisha; there Carmel and the place of Elijah's sacrifice . . .'

There is one brief reference to Megiddo in the book of Revelation where Armageddon means the Hill of Megiddo (Revelation 16:14–16). The Apostle John describes a great battle between the armies of the world on the final day of the Lord. It is possible that this portrays a literal battle or is perhaps a symbolic reference to the final overthrow of evil by God.

At a time when there is much foreboding about the future, Megiddo reminds us to put our hope in the sovereignty of God who rules over history, not in our intellectual genius, military strength or financial resources (Jeremiah 9:23–24).

THE STABLES, BUILT BY EITHER SOLOMON OR AHAB

A View
of the
Megiddo/
Jezreel
Plain

The River Jordan

Lot looked up and saw that the whole plain of the Jordan was well watered, like the garden of the LORD, like the land of Egypt, towards Zoar. (Genesis 13:10)

In Hebrew, Jordan (Yarden), means 'the descender'. This is because it flows through the Jordan Valley from the snowy slopes of Mount Hermon, the highest peak in the Orient, down to the Dead Sea, the lowest place on earth. It is the lowest river on earth, flowing for most of its course below sea level. Whereas the distance from Mount Hermon to the Dead Sea is 113 kilometres, the length of the Jordan River, as it meanders through the valley, is actually 323 kilometres.

The Jordan has three principal sources: the first is the Leddan which flows from the base of the hillside near the ancient border town of Dan. The second source, called the Banyas, flows from under the limestone cliffs near the ruins of Caesarea Philippi joining the Leddan about nine kilometres south of Dan. The third source is called the Hasbany which rises on the western slopes of Mount Hermon and joins the main stream about two kilometres further south. Here the river is about 15 metres wide and flows through a deep channel 4 to 5 metres deep before it enters the Sea of Galilee. For most of its length the Jordan is between 28 and 31 metres wide and between 1 and 3 metres deep. Because there are 27 sets of rapids along the river it carries no traffic. Although there were a number of fords between the Sea of Galilee and the Dead Sea, it was not until the arrival of the Romans that the river was bridged.

There are two important tributaries which enter the River Jordan further south, between the Sea of Galilee and the Dead Sea. The Yarmuk formed the boundary between Bashan and Gilead, and the Jabbok which enters the Jordan about 30 kilometres north of Jericho was formerly the northern boundary of Ammon.

JORDAN RIVER, NORTH OF SEA OF GALILEE

Led by Joshua, the Israelites miraculously crossed the flooded Jordan, probably near Adam, 26 kilometres north of Jericho, 'on dry land' (Joshua 3:15–17). God later enabled both Elijah and Elisha to repeat the miracle (2 Kings 2:8,14). Naaman was healed in its waters (2 Kings 5:8–14) and David crossed it to escape from his rebellious son Absalom (2 Samuel 17:22–24). The importance of the Jordan River in Scripture is because it was regarded as a natural border, not just between the eastern and western tribes of Israel (Numbers 34:10–12), but also, as the River Jordan features most significantly in the ministry of John the Baptist and in the baptism of the Lord Jesus (Matthew 3:6; Mark 1:9–11).

To cross the Jordan became figurative of making a decision, like crossing the Rubicon (Deuteronomy 3:18–20; 27:4; Joshua 1:2). Is there a 'Jordan' that you must cross metaphorically, in obedience to God, in order that you too may experience his blessings and receive your inheritance?

Surrounded by mountains, the entire valley is in a rain shadow from the westerly rain-bearing winds. Average annual rainfall at Dan is about 600 mm. The Sea of Galilee receives about 400mm, whereas at Jericho on average only 125 mm falls each year. In biblical times the Jordan Valley was full of dense vegetation and in many places was also swampy, the habitat of lions and other wild animals (Jeremiah 12:5; 50:44; Zechariah 11:3). It is probably for a combination of these reasons that no large city ever grew up on the banks of the Jordan.

The Jordan did however play a significant role in the history of Israel and is mentioned 178 times in the Old Testament and 15 in the New Testament. It is first referred to in the story of Abraham and Lot when they separated and shared the land between them (Genesis 13:8–12). Jacob crossed the Jordan on several occasions (Genesis 32:10), wrestling with the Lord at the ford of the Jabbok (Genesis 32:22–30).

JORDAN RIVER, SOUTH OF SEA OF GALILEE

THE RIVER
JORDAN AS
IT FLOWS
INTO THE
SEA OF
GALILEE

Bethlehem

'But you, Bethlehem Ephrathah, though you are small among the clans of Judah, out of you will come for me one who will be ruler over Israel, whose origins are from of old, from ancient times.' (Micah 5:2)

The first occasion in which Bethlehem is mentioned in history has been found in the Amarna letters written from tribal kings of Palestine to the Egyptian pharaohs, probably sometime between 1400–1360 BC. The ruler in Jerusalem complains that *Bit-Lahmi* has deserted to the '*Apiru*' people, a word probably referring to the Hebrews.

Originally called Ephrath, meaning 'fruitful' (Genesis 35:16-19), Bethlehem itself means 'house of bread' and it is not hard to see why. Situated about eight kilometres south of Jerusalem and 750 metres above sea level, Bethlehem commands a strategic location on a ridge running north–south along the watershed of the Judean highlands, dividing the barren desert wilderness of the Jordan Valley to the east from the fertile coastal plain to the west.

The slopes on this western side toward Beit Jala abound with figs, almonds and olives. They are still renowned for their vineyards. To the east lies Beit Sahour which means the Shepherd's Fields. To the south is the ancient road from Jerusalem to Hebron and Egypt.

The town of Bethlehem is mentioned frequently in the Bible. Its location became sacred when Jacob buried his beloved wife Rachel by the road side near the northern entrance to Bethlehem. (Genesis 35:19; 48:7). It is possible that Salma, the son of Caleb, built the first Jewish settlement there (1 Chronicles 2:51). The town and surrounding fields

CHURCHES AND MOSQUES CROWD THE CENTRE OF BETHLEHEM

also feature prominently in the romantic love story of Ruth and Boaz who became the great-grandparents of David (Ruth 1; 2:4; 4:11). The town grew in prominence when Samuel anointed the shepherd boy David, to be king of Israel there (1 Samuel 16:4–13).

Following their exile in Babylon only 123 men returned to live in Bethlehem (Ezra 2:21). However, the prophet Micah predicted an even more glorious future because one greater than David, indeed the Saviour of the world, eternal in origin and universal in significance, would also be born there (Micah 5:2). When the Magi came from the East searching for the one to be born king of the Jews, Herod consulted with the chief priests and biblical scholars, who it seems knew full well the significance of Micah's prophecy (Matthew 2:1-8; John 7:42). By New Testament times Bethlehem had come to be known as 'The town of David' (Luke 2:4,11).

The New Testament records in great simplicity and humility how that amazing prophecy came true in the lowly birth of the Son of God (Matthew 2; Luke 2; John 7:42). The traditional and undisputed site is found in a cave beneath what is now probably the oldest surviving church in the world, the Church of the Nativity in Manger Square.

In the silence of this ancient site, best visited in the early morning, it is possible to pause and worship near the place where the Lord Jesus Christ was born. To enter the church one must first stoop low below the lintel. The tallest must stoop the furthest, only children can enter without bending down. What a lesson in humility.

The tragic fulfilment of another prophecy is remembered nearby in a chapel dedicated to the little boys murdered by Herod in his mad and futile attempt to kill the legitimate King of the Jews (Jeremiah 31:15; Matthew 2:16–18).

The bleak and weathered hills on which the lowly shepherds encountered the heavenly angels that first Christmas, though ravaged by centuries of military occupation and human suffering, continue to bear silent witness to our world's desperate need of redemption, of a Saviour who is Christ the Lord.

Bethlehem is therefore unique. It is the place where Almighty God, the Creator of the universe, entered our world and became a human being. For many, Bethlehem and the Christmas story is the place where they first begin to experience the meaning of that enigmatic phrase 'He has also set eternity in the hearts of men. . .' (Ecclesiastes 3:11), for here in this place time, eternity and destiny meet in Jesus. It is hard to comprehend the wonder and enormity of this fact. Words cannot improve on the declaration of the angels to the shepherds, *'Today in the town of David a Saviour has been born to you; he is Christ the Lord.'* (Luke 2:11).

How appropriate that the One who said 'I am the Bread of Life' should be born in the house of bread. On another occasion Jesus said, *"Whoever eats my flesh and drinks my blood has eternal life, and I will raise him up at the last day. For my flesh is real food and my blood is real drink'.* (John 6:54–55). Let us indeed feed on him in our hearts by faith with thanksgiving.

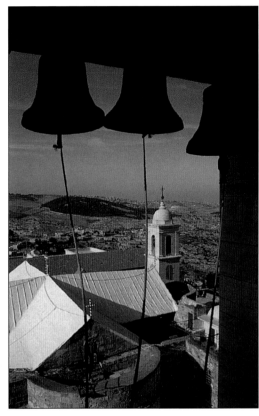

THE BELL TOWER OF THE CHURCH OF THE NATIVITY

SHEPHERDS'
FIELDS,
BETHLEHEM

41

The Hills of Galilee

When Jesus heard that John had been put in prison, he returned to Galilee. Leaving Nazareth, he went and lived in Capernaum, which was by the lake in the area of Zebulun and Naphtali – to fulfil what was said through the prophet Isaiah:'Land of Zebulun and land of Naphtali, the way to the sea, along the Jordan, Galilee of the Gentiles – the people living in darkness have seen a great light; on those living in the land of the shadow of death a light has dawned.' (Matthew 4:12–16)

WESTERN SHORES, SEA OF GALILEE

Galilee means 'a ring' or 'circuit'. The term is used of the region extending from the Litani River in Lebanon in the north to the Valley of Jezreel in the south, and from the Mediterranean coast in the west to the Jordan River in the east. The region 1,000 metres above sea level is known as Upper Galilee and lies to the north of a line from the Bay of Acco to the Sea of Galilee. In the first century this region was sparsely populated and densely wooded. The region to the south below 1000 metres above sea level is known as Lower Galilee and includes the Jezreel Valley. Here the climate is milder, the soil richer and the population was more dense. Josephus says that in the first century there were 204 villages in Galilee.

The first occasion when Galilee appears in the Bible is in the context of *'The king of Goyim in Gilgal'* (Joshua 12:23), which may best be translated as *'king of the nations of Galilee'*. This reveals the presence of distinct ethnic groups living in Galilee alongside the Israelite tribes of Naphtali, Asher, Issachar and Zebulun, and later, Dan. So, under the Monarchy, when Solomon needed to pay Hiram for supplies of wood and gold used in the construction of the Temple in Jerusalem, he offered him 20 towns in Galilee as

LANDSCAPE WEST OF SEA OF GALILEE

collateral (1 Kings 9:10-14; 2 Chronicles 8:1-2). Hiram did not regard them of sufficient value and it appears Solomon later settled his debt and recovered the towns when his reserves had been replenished.

About the year 732 BC Tiglath-Pileser, the king of Assyria, deported the Israelites living in Galilee. He replaced them with people from Babylon and Syria (2 Kings 15:29; 17:24). It is probably for this reason Isaiah describes the area as '*Galilee of the Gentiles*', since it was a cosmopolitan mix of Jews, Aramaeans, Ituraeans, Phoenicians and Greeks. It seems Galilee was in some ways a melting pot of different ethnic groups (Isaiah 9:1; Matthew 4:15).

In consequence Galilee developed a reputation for independence and rebellion against authority (Luke 13:1; Acts 5:37). Galileans also evolved their own distinctive accent (Matthew 26:69, 73) and came to be despised by the more legalistic Jews of Judea in the south. For example, when Nicodemus defended Jesus before the Sanhedrin they replied sarcastically, '*Are you from Galilee too? Look into it, and you will find that a prophet does not come out of Galilee*' (John 7:52). Their arrogance toward Galileans distorted their historical perspective for the prophet Jonah, and probably Nahum and Hosea all came from Galilee.

It is most significant that Jesus chose to base most of his ministry in Galilee. The hills and villages of Galilee provided a dramatic backdrop for much of the gospel story. Capernaum, for instance, became his home town (Matthew 9:1). Jesus performed his first miracle at the wedding in Cana and his last by the Sea of Galilee (John 2:11; 21:4–12). Indeed 25 of his 33 recorded miracles were performed here. Likewise 19 of his 32 parables were spoken in Galilee. This may have been because Galilee gave Jesus access to the rest of the Roman Empire and beyond. Conveniently, the Via Maris, the international highway from Egypt to Syria, passed along the northern shore near Capernaum. Galilee also enjoyed comparative religious freedom from the priestly and pharisaical legalism and prejudice found in Jerusalem.

Galilee was a microcosm of the world. Jesus made his home there, equipped his disciples and developed his strategy to reach the entire world from the 'Galilee of the Gentiles'. We all live in our own Galilee with its multi-cultural tensions, its ethical challenges and gospel opportunities. Jesus calls us to break down the barriers in our world, overcome our narrow prejudices and share his liberating message in word and deed with everyone we meet, irrespective of their gender, race or culture. Our Lord's words to his first disciples are as much our own mandate too. '*A new command I give you: Love one another. As I have loved you, so you must love one another. By this all men will know that you are my disciples, if you love one another.*' (John 13:34–35)

Hills above Sea of Galilee

43

Nazareth

In the sixth month, God sent the angel Gabriel to Nazareth, a town in Galilee, to a virgin pledged to be married to a man named Joseph, a descendant of David. The virgin's name was Mary. (Luke 1:26–27)

Nazareth is nestled in a hollow valley high up among the hills of lower Galilee overlooking the broad and flat Jezreel Valley. It is about halfway between the Sea of Galilee and the Mediterranean.

Caravans on the main trade routes from Egypt, Ptolemais, Gilead and Damascus passed through the valley within a few kilometres of Nazareth. The frequent movement of foreign armies would also have been observed from there at a safe distance. Given its commanding view, it is likely that 'Nazareth' is derived from the Aramaic, meaning 'watch tower' although it is possibly a derivation of the Hebrew for 'shoot'.

Nazareth is not mentioned in either the Old Testament or Talmud. It is first referred to in the Gospels as the home of Mary and Joseph, and the place where Jesus grew up (Matthew 13:53–57; Luke 4:16). Perhaps Joseph felt Jesus would be safe from Archelaus in such a small and relatively obscure community (Matthew 2:21–23). As a growing young man, Jesus met with favour and respect within his community (Luke 2:51–52).

THE FRONT ENTRANCE TO THE STRIKING MODERN CHURCH OF THE ANNUNCIATION

A GENERAL VIEW OF THE TOWN OF NAZARETH

Nazareth may have been regarded as an insignificant or even a dubious place to live, its residents perhaps distinguished by their 'northern' accent. Whatever the reason, Nathanael is initially scornful when told that the Messiah is from Nazareth (John 1:46). Similarly the religious leaders, not knowing the birth of Jesus in Bethlehem, were sceptical about his association with Nazareth (John 7:41–43, 52).

Jesus began his public ministry in Nazareth. He had regularly attended the synagogue there but on this occasion, reading from the scroll of Isaiah predicting the coming of the Messiah, Jesus said, 'Today this scripture is fulfilled in your hearing' (Isaiah 61:1–2; Luke 4:16–21). Thinking that they knew him, their response to his claim was one of hostility and rejection (Luke 4:28–30). On a second occasion Jesus returned to his home town and taught in their synagogue (Matthew 13:54–57). But because of their continued unbelief Jesus was unable to perform many miracles (Matthew 13:58). Although known as 'Jesus of Nazareth' (Luke 18:37; 24:19) the saddest day for that community must have been the day Jesus left Nazareth and made Capernaum his home while living in Galilee (Matthew 4:13; 10:13–15).

Nazareth reminds us that it is so easy to despise the familiar; to fail to appreciate or to take for granted things like our homes and families or even God's presence with us. Like the people of Nazareth we may not notice the ways God is intervening in our world, every day, speaking his will into our own personal situations, just as he did that very ordinary day when Mary heard the angel say, 'Greetings, you who are highly favoured! The Lord is with you' (Luke 1:28).

It is not for us to question or try and work out 'how' God's will may be accomplished, but like Mary, our part is to respond in simple trust, 'I am the Lord's servant . . . May it be to me as you have said' (Luke 1:38). And then by God's grace, it most surely will.

HAR NAZARETH, THE HILL JUST OUTSIDE THE TOWN OF NAZARETH

Cana of Galilee

'Everyone brings out the choice wine first and then the cheaper wine after the guests have had too much to drink; but you have saved the best till now.' This, the first of his miraculous signs, Jesus performed in Cana of Galilee. He thus revealed his glory, and his disciples put their faith in him. (John 2:10–11)

ROMAN MOSAIC OF WATER CARRIER

Cana means *'place of reeds'* suggesting something of the beautiful countryside of lower Galilee. It is distinguished from the other biblical Cana in Lebanon mentioned in Joshua 19 verse 28, by the designation *'Cana of Galilee'*. Cana survives today as a small town on the tourist road between Nazareth and the Sea of Galilee, just as it was when Jesus took his mother and family and friends 'down' to the lakeside at Capernaum, perhaps for a few days' rest (John 2:12).

Cana was the home of Nathanael, one of the apostles (John 21:2). Although Cana is only mentioned in John's Gospel, it is remembered above all as the place where Jesus performed his first great miraculous 'sign' (John 2:1–11). On another occasion Jesus

BELL TOWER OF THE GREEK CHURCH, CANA

visited the town and encountered a royal official desperate for Jesus to heal his son who was dying. Although Jesus rebukes the people for seeking *'miraculous signs and wonders'* (John 4:48), in compassion and simply by the spoken word, he performs a second miracle in Cana and the boy is healed instantaneously even though he is many miles away in Capernaum.

How appropriate that the divine 'Bridegroom' (Isaiah 62:5; John 3:29; Matthew 9:15), should reveal his glory at a humble wedding. In the days of Jesus, the bridegroom would walk to the house of his bride and they would walk back together to his house followed by their families. The whole town was involved in the procession. When the couple arrived at the groom's house, the reception would take place with plenty of food and wine. Usually the party would last for several days. That is why it was always possible to run out of food or wine. Jesus turned the water into wine, not just to save the couple from embarrassment; it was a sign of what he had come to do for us all.

FRANCISCAN CHURCH, CANA

come from. Perhaps they too became disciples of Christ, at least after the honeymoon.

Jesus' power to turn water into wine, is a picture of his work in us, the Church, his 'Bride'. Jesus has the power to change our ordinary lives into something special by his presence, his provision and power. The Bible uses the word 'metamorphosis' to describe this amazing transformation (Romans 12:1–2). The 'sign' miracles of Jesus, and this was the first, were not performed to trick or entertain, but to prove that God had come in the person of Jesus to share his joy and love and enable us to know him as our Friend and Saviour.

AMPHORAS USED FOR STORING VARIOUS PRODUCTS

Jesus blessed the couple and their community in three specific ways. First he blessed them with his presence, but he needed to be invited. Second, Jesus blessed them with his provision. The six stone water jars held between 120 and 180 gallons which is a lot of wine and it was very good wine at that. Jesus blessed them with quantity and quality, but Mary had to ask him. Third, Jesus blessed them with his power for this was not simply an act of compassion or generosity. It was a supernatural miracle and John points out that as a consequence, *'his disciples put their faith in him'*. I wonder about the bride and groom. They must have also known where the wine had

VIEW OVER
CANA IN
GALILEE

53

Capernaum

After Jesus and his disciples arrived in Capernaum … the disciples came to Jesus and asked, 'Who is the greatest in the kingdom of heaven?' He called a little child and had him stand among them. And he said: 'I tell you the truth, unless you change and become like little children, you will never enter the kingdom of heaven. Therefore, whoever humbles himself like this child is the greatest in the kingdom of heaven. And whoever welcomes a little child like this in my name welcomes me.' (Matthew 17:24, 18:1–5)

SYNAGOGUE, CAPERNAUM

Capernaum is situated on the scenic north-western shore of the Sea of Galilee. This important city, mentioned only in the Gospels, is on the ancient Via Maris, the main international trade route from the Mediterranean coastal plain through the Golan Heights on to Damascus and the East. It is also situated near where the fresh water of the River Jordan, carrying the melted snows of Mount Hermon, enters Galilee. Since the many varieties of fish are attracted to the fresh water, Capernaum came to dominate the thriving fishing communities along the northern shore of this border region, most likely after the return of the Jews from captivity.

This perhaps explains the presence of a Roman tax and customs post as well as a military base under the command of a centurion (Luke 5:27) who also apparently built the synagogue there, the foundations of which are still visible today (Luke 7:1–5). These are probably the reasons why Capernaum is described as a 'city' in the original Greek of the Gospels (Matthew 9:1; Mark 1:21) to distinguish it from the smaller fishing villages nearby such as Bethsaida and Magdala.

STONE CORNICE (DETAIL) SYNAGOGUE, CAPERNAUM

CAPERNAUM AND THE SEA OF GALILEE

mother-in-law (Luke 4:38–39). The scene portrayed by Matthew, Mark and Luke of the whole town gathered at the door of Peter's home, as the sun was going down, is one of the most moving in the New Testament. According to Mark, Jesus continued to minister long after it was dark. *That evening after sunset the people brought to Jesus all the sick and demon-possessed. The whole town gathered at the door . . .'* (Mark 1:32–33). Yet his first priority in Capernaum, as elsewhere, was to teach and preach about the kingdom of God (Mark 1:38–39). Although Jesus used Capernaum as his home base, many of the people who lived there did not understand his message and tried unsuccessfully to make him king by force (John 6:14–15).

The message of Capernaum? It is futile trying to make Jesus fit our expectations or our agenda for him. Unless we change and become like little children, we too like those of Capernaum, will never enter the kingdom of heaven (Luke 10:15–16).

Capernaum was therefore a strategic location for the development of Jesus' ministry. It was known as the 'Galilee of the Gentiles' (Isaiah 9:1). Matthew sees great significance in this, indeed as the fulfilment of Isaiah's prophecy of the coming Messiah (Matthew 4:13–16). It is not surprising perhaps that when he was rejected in Nazareth Jesus made Capernaum his 'home'. He probably stayed with Peter and his family (Mark 2:1; Luke 4:38–40). Jesus chose several of his disciples from among its residents, including Matthew the tax collector and fishermen such as Simon Peter and his brother Andrew (Matthew 9:9; Mark 1:29).

Jesus frequently taught in the synagogue at Capernaum (Mark 1:21–22; John 6:25–59). Many of his miracles were also performed here, like the healing of the centurion's servant (Matthew 8:5; Luke 7:1–2), the man possessed by a demon (Mark 1:23–28) and Simon's

STONE CORNICE, CAPERNAUM

The Sea of Galilee

SUNSET, SEA OF GALILEE

As Jesus was walking beside the Sea of Galilee, he saw two brothers, Simon called Peter and his brother Andrew. They were casting a net into the lake, for they were fishermen. 'Come, follow me,' Jesus said, 'and I will make you fishers of men.' (Matthew 4:18–19)

The Sea of Galilee is known by four different names in the Bible. In the Old Testament it is first called the 'Sea of Kinnereth' probably because it is harp-shaped (Numbers 34:11; Joshua 12:3). In the New Testament Luke alone calls it the 'Lake of Gennesaret' (Luke 5:1). Matthew and Mark call it the 'Sea of Galilee' and John twice calls it the 'Sea of Tiberias' (John 6:1; 21:1). The Sea of Galilee, at 211 metres below sea level, is the lowest freshwater lake in the world. At its widest the lake is 13 kilometres from east to west and 22 kilometres from north to south, forming part of the geological fault which runs from Syria to Africa. Within this rift, the River Jordan flows down from Mount Hermon bringing fresh water into the Sea of Galilee near Capernaum on the northern shore and flows out in the south near Yardenit on its way to the Dead Sea.

Hills surround the lake like a horseshoe on the west, north and eastern sides. These are between 360 and 450 metres high and, because the lake itself is below sea level, abrupt changes in temperature can occur. This causes strong winds to sweep down without warning,

BOAT ON THE SEA OF GALILEE

SUNRISE, SEA OF GALILEE

leading to violent storms and turbulent waves. The Gospels record several storms which Jesus and the disciples encountered while on the lake (Matthew 8:23–27; 14:22–34).

In the first century AD the great abundance of fish and shellfish found in the lake attracted a large population in an almost continuous belt of settlements along its northern shore. Important fishing towns of more than 15,000 residents included Capernaum and Bethsaida, which means 'house of fish'. Conveniently, the Via Maris, the international highway from Egypt to Syria, passed along the northern shore near Capernaum. Around 40 different varieties of fish live in the lake. The most popular, Tilapia, is better known now as 'Peter's fish' and these and other species were salted and exported all over the Roman Empire. Jesus chose Simon Peter and his brother Andrew, together with James and his brother John from among the fishermen of Galilee to be his disciples. He promised they would become 'fishers of men' (Matthew 4:18–22; Luke 5:1–11). The Sea of Galilee is associated with some of the most dramatic miracles Jesus performed, such as the stilling of the storm (Matthew 8:23–27), the feeding of the 5,000 (Matthew 14:15–21), and the exorcism of the demoniac of Gerasene (Luke 8:26–39). Here too, by the lakeside, the Lord revealed himself to the disciples after his resurrection (John 21). Jesus made use of a fishing net to illustrate what it will be like on the day of judgement when the kingdom of heaven is revealed (Matthew 13:47–50) as had the prophet Ezekiel previously (Ezekiel 32:3). The Sea of Galilee was indeed the cradle of the gospel.

The hills surrounding the Sea of Galilee are spectacular, and it is easy to imagine Jesus with you there, especially when the sun is shining, glittering on the surface of the lake. But you don't have to visit the Sea of Galilee to discover that Jesus is with you and able to still your storms today. Simply see your circumstances, however bleak, from his perspective, allow him full command of your situation; obey his Word and witness his miraculous intervention.

FISHERMAN
REPAIRING NETS

Hermon

It is as if the dew of Hermon were falling on Mount Zion. For there the LORD bestows his blessing, even life for evermore. (Psalm 133:3)

MOUNT HERMON, SPRINGTIME

SLOPES OF MOUNT HERMON

From earliest times Hermon was regarded as a holy place (Psalm 89:12). In Hebrew, Hermon means 'sanctuary', a sacred or forbidden place. It was known as 'Sirion' among the Phoenicians and 'Senir' among the Amorites (Deuteronomy 3:8–9). The mountain was also called 'Baal-Hermon' in the time of Joshua and the Judges, indicating that it was a sacred place of worship prior to the Hebrew conquest (Judges 3:3). Mount Hermon marked the northern boundary for the people of Israel (Joshua 11:16–17; 12:1).

The Greeks later worshipped the god Pan there and named the town on its southern slope 'Paneas'. Herod the Great built a marble temple to Augustus Caesar there and Philip the tetrarch renamed the town Caesarea Philippi. In the time of Christ Caesarea Philippi was largely a Gentile frontier town.

Mount Hermon actually comprises three peaks and is the highest mountain in the Levant rising to 2,814 metres. Large quantities of precipitation fall on the mountain, as much as 1,000 metres per year, mostly in the form of snow. The upper slopes remain covered virtually all year. Hermon is the primary source for the Jordan and also feeds the Litani River as well as the Oasis of Damascus. In clear weather, Mount Hermon is visible from great distances. It dominates the landscape. From the Mediterranean Coastal Plain to the Jordan Valley, the snow-capped cone forms the one permanent feature on the northern horizon of Israel. In biblical times the slopes were apparently covered in thick forests, and a home for lions and leopards (Ezekiel 27:5; Songs of Songs 4:8).

It is very likely that Mount Hermon is the 'high mountain' on which the Lord Jesus Christ was transfigured (Matthew 17:1–9);

THE ARID SLOPES OF MOUNT HERMON ON THE EASTERN SIDE FACING THE GOLAN HEIGHTS

Mountains like Hermon help give us a wider perspective, and to locate ourselves. They are a security, places associated with retreat and prayer (Mark 3:13). Their age and size make us aware of our own mortality and God's awesome creative power (Psalm 36:5–6). While in exile, David reflected on the depths of the Jordan and the heights of Hermon. They were for him symbols of the source and extent of God's blessing, his love and protection (Psalm 42:5–11; 133:3).

The word used to describe the transfiguration of Jesus is 'metamorphosis'. Amazingly, the same word is used of Christians who are being made like Jesus (Romans 12:1–2). Hermon is a reminder then not only of the transfiguration of Jesus but also of the fact that 'we, who with unveiled faces all reflect the Lord's glory, are being transformed into his likeness with ever-increasing glory' (2 Corinthians 3:18).

Therefore we are not discouraged by adversity for we realise that 'though outwardly we are wasting away, yet inwardly we are being renewed day by day. For our light and momentary troubles are achieving for us an eternal glory that far outweighs them all. So we fix our eyes not on what is seen, but on what is unseen. For what is seen is temporary, but what is unseen is eternal' (2 Corinthians 4:16–18).

MOUNT HERMON AND HULA VALLEY FROM HAR GERSHOM

Mark 9:2–9; Luke 9:28–37). In the days before, he and his disciples had been ministering in the villages around Caesarea Philippi on the slopes of Mount Hermon. It was also here that Jesus asked his disciples who they thought he was (Matthew 16:13–20). Peter's affirmation that Jesus was indeed 'the Christ, the Son of the living God' (Matthew 16:16), was then confirmed by the dramatic events on the mountain. Peter, James and John were privileged not only to see the Lord Jesus in his eternal glory but also to hear Almighty God affirm that: 'This is my Son, whom I love; with him I am well pleased. Listen to him!' (Matthew 17:5).

MOUNT
HERMON

65

Caesarea Philippi

When Jesus came to the region of Caesarea Philippi, he asked his disciples, 'Who do people say the Son of Man is?' They replied, 'Some say John the Baptist; others say Elijah; and still others, Jeremiah or one of the prophets.' 'But what about you?' he asked. 'Who do you say I am?' Simon Peter answered, 'You are the Christ, the Son of the living God.' Jesus replied, 'Blessed are you, Simon son of Jonah, for this was not revealed to you by man, but by my Father in heaven.' (Matthew 16:13–17)

Caesarea Philippi is situated high up in the Golan Heights on the south-western slope of Mount Hermon, about 190 kilometres from Jerusalem and 80 kilometres from Damascus. It commands a strategic position on the main road through the Golan, dominating the valleys of northern Galilee below. From a cave at the foot of a steep bluff on the northern edge of the city flows one of the two sources of the River Jordan. For these reasons from earliest times, Caesarea Philippi has been a major centre for pagan worship.

Earliest records suggest it was a Canaanite sanctuary and perhaps the site of Baal-Hermon and the worship of the fertility god Baal (Judges 3:3; 1 Chronicles 5:23). A major battle took place here in 198 BC when the Egyptian army was defeated by the Seleucids under Antiochus the Great. During this time of Greek ascendancy in Palestine the site became an important centre for the worship of the god Pan and so was renamed Paneas.

The region eventually fell to the Romans and in 20 BC the emperor Augustus bequeathed Paneas to Herod the Great. Herod built a pagan temple of white marble here dedicated to Augustus Caesar in appreciation of his benefactor. When Herod died, his son Philip became tetrarch and in 4 BC rebuilt the city. He renamed it

ROCK NICHE AT THE TEMPLE TO PAN

66

Caesarea Philippi in deference to Augustus Caesar. He also added his own name to distinguish it from the other Caesarea on the Mediterranean coast. Herod Agrippa II, grandson of Herod the Great, subsequently changed its name to Neronias in honour of the emperor Nero. Still later, having put down the Jewish revolt, the Romans changed the name back to Paneas once again. Today the Syrian village, occupied by Israel since 1967, is known by its Arabic name, Banyas.

Two niches cut into the face of the rock beside the cave are all that remain of its idolatrous origins. Caesarea Philippi is best remembered, however, as the place where the Lord Jesus Christ was revealed to be the Son of God. Six days after Jesus affirmed Peter's great confession, he was miraculously transfigured, probably nearby on Mount Hermon, meeting with Moses and Elijah, before his stunned disciples, Peter, James and John (Matthew 16:13–17:13). This high and remote region was a most appropriate place for Jesus to take his disciples on retreat to prepare them for his imminent humiliation, crucifixion and, afterwards, his triumphant resurrection. The transfiguration of Jesus gave a brief glimpse of his true eternal glory, laid aside when he came to earth but restored after his ascension (Philippians 2:5–11). On the basis of Peter's confession that Jesus was the Messiah, it was here in Caesarea Philippi, that Jesus also first revealed his purpose for the Church '...*on this rock I will build my church, and the gates of Hades will not overcome it*' (Matthew 16:18).

So it was at Caesarea Philippi then that Jesus asked his disciples the most important question they would ever face. '*Who do you say that I am?*' It is the same ultimate question we must answer if we too are to be transformed and become like Jesus. '*And we, who with unveiled faces all reflect the Lord's glory, are being transformed into his likeness with ever-increasing glory*' (2 Corinthians 3:12–18; Romans 12:1–2).

BANYAS SPRING AT THE TEMPLE TO PAN

Samaria

Now [Jesus] had to go through Samaria. So he came to a town in Samaria called Sychar, near the plot of ground Jacob had given to his son Joseph. Jacob's well was there, and Jesus, tired as he was from the journey, sat down by the well. It was about the sixth hour. (John 4:4–6)

Samaria means 'a watch-mountain' or 'watch-tower'. This apposite name refers to the mountainous region, sandwiched between the secular Galilee of the Gentiles in the north and the religious orthodoxy of Jerusalem and Judea to the south. The name was also given to the hilltop city founded by King Omri, the father

TEMPLE OF AUGUSTUS

of Ahab, after the former owner Shemer, whose name means 'watch' (1 Kings 16:24). This imposing location became the capital of the northern kingdom after Solomon's death. Samaria is a beautiful and diverse region of mountains and valleys.

With good supplies of rain, olives grow in abundance along with vines, grain and citrus fruits. Strategically situated on important ancient highways near the ancient well dug by Jacob, the city of Samaria gave access to Jerusalem to the south, Megiddo and the Jezreel Valley to the north, as well as to the sea and coastal plain to the west, and the Jordan Valley and Phoenicia to the east.

Under the influence of Jezebel and Ahab, Samaria became a notorious centre for idolatrous worship. The Hebrew Prophets repeatedly called on the people of Samaria to repent, graphically warning of judgement for their pride and arrogance (Isaiah 9:8-17), their wickedness (Hosea 7:1–7), rebellion (Hosea 13:16), and exploitation of the poor (Amos 3:9–12; 4:1–3). The city was destroyed and rebuilt on many occasions, its population deported and resettled by waves of Assyrians, Greeks and Romans. It was this mixed community of Jews and Gentiles, known as Samaritans, who in the Hellenistic period built a replica of the Temple to the Hebrew God on Mount Gerizim to rival that in Jerusalem. This was later destroyed by John Hyrcanus around 128 BC. It is something of an

VIEW FROM SAMARIA

understatement to say that by the time of Christ, the relationship between the Jews and the Samaritans was strained (Luke 9:51–56; John 8:48–51). The animosity was so deep that the Jews would avoid passing through Samaria on their journey between Galilee and Judea. They would rather take a wide detour to the east, cross the Jordan River and travel through barren and inhospitable Gentile territory if it meant they could avoid contact with Samaritans.

That is why Jesus' attitude towards Samaritans is so remarkable, so free from the ugly racism as common then as today. Jesus openly rebuked his disciples for their hostility towards the Samaritans when rejected by them (Luke 9:55-56). On one memorable occasion Jesus told a story that exalted a Samaritan for his compassion in contrast to the indifference of representatives of his own people (Luke 10:25-27).

On another occasion it was a Samaritan leper whom he praises for his thankfulness, lamenting the ungratefulness of the other nine who were presumably Jews (Luke 17:11–19). Significantly, Jesus intentionally travelled through Samaria (John 4:4), stopped at Jacob's well and asked a Samaritan woman for a drink (John 4:7) to the amazement of his disciples, and then preached the gospel to her community so that many Samaritans responded gladly (John 4:39–42). When in Acts 1:8, the risen Christ commanded his disciples to witness specifically in Samaria, Philip, Peter and John obeyed and many Samaritans came to faith in Jesus Christ (Acts 8:4–17; 15:3).

Samaria, perhaps more than any other location in the Holy Land reminds us of the patience and mercy of God. Its message rebukes our tendency to avoid or discriminate against people because of their race, colour or creed. How often are we, like the disciples, eager to call down fire from heaven upon those who give us a hard time? Samaria emphasises the universality of the gospel and the inclusiveness of God's Kingdom.

WEST GATE, SAMARIA

THE STEPS OF THE TEMPLE OF AUGUSTUS

View from Sebaste (Ancient Samaria)

Jericho

Then they came to Jericho. As Jesus and his disciples, together with a large crowd, were leaving the city, a blind man, Bartimaeus (that is, the Son of Timaeus), was sitting by the roadside begging. When he heard that it was Jesus of Nazareth, he began to shout, 'Jesus, Son of David, have mercy on me.' (Mark 10:46–47)

JERICHO FROM MONASTERY OF TEMPTATION

There are three sites on which Jericho was built at different times in history. The conical mound of Tel Jericho represents all that remains of the earliest settlements. Just to the east where the Wadi Qelt emerges from the Judean wilderness into the Jordan Valley lie the foundations of first-century Jericho with its royal winter palaces of the Hasmonean and Herodian period. Modern Crusader Jericho is a short walk to the south and is visible for great distances because of the abundance of its trees and rich green vegetation.

NEOLITHIC STONE TOWER (8000 BC)

Jericho is situated in the broad and fertile Jordan Plain, opposite Mount Nebo (Deuteronomy 32:49), ten kilometres north of the Dead Sea and at 240 metres below sea level, the lowest city on earth. The climate is tropical, which, combined with the rich alluvial soil, the presence of a perennial spring and the proximity of the Jordan River, has created an oasis justly earning Jericho the accolade 'city of palms' (Deuteronomy 34:3). A historic east–west road which fords the River Jordan nearby also makes Jericho a strategic entry point into Palestine (Joshua 3:14–17). It is probably for these reasons that Jericho is the oldest known inhabited city in the world. The earliest

remains are dated to around 7,000 years BC so that by the time the Hebrew tribes emerged from the wilderness, Jericho was already an ancient and prosperous city defended by stone walls built on an earthen embankment. The name Jericho is associated with the worship of the semitic fertility cult moon-god Yarih.

Given its strategic location, the most important settlement in the Jordan Valley, Jericho features prominently in the story of the settlement of Palestine by the Israelites. After Jericho was destroyed by the Israelites, no attempt was made to rebuild the city for 400 years and the site remained uninhabited (Joshua 6:24–26). During this long period of abandonment the remains of the fallen city walls and buildings were exposed to the weather and eroded, making their dating within the archaeological strata difficult. Jericho was eventually rebuilt by Hiel of Bethel in the reign of King Ahab. The curse placed by Joshua on anyone re-establishing the city was fulfilled in the death of his eldest and youngest sons (1 Kings 16:34). In the time of Elijah and Elisha, Jericho was the home for a school of prophets (2 Kings 2:4–5; 18–22). The plains of Jericho also feature in the sad story of the capture of Zedekiah, the last king of Judah, by the Babylonians (2 Kings 25:5–7).

Jesus visited Jericho on a number of occasions. The traditional site where he was baptised by John in the Jordan River is near Jericho (Matthew 3:5–17). Similarly his temptation may have taken place in the Judean wilderness to the west of the city (Matthew 4:1–11). Jewish pilgrims travelling to Jerusalem from Galilee who wished to avoid Samaria would travel via Jericho. On occasions Jesus also used this route (Matthew 20:17–19; 20–29; 21:2). In Jericho Jesus called people like Zacchaeus, the tax collector, to become his disciples, and demonstrated his Messianic claims and supernatural power by giving sight to the blind (Mark 10:46–52). Some of his parables such as the 'Good Samaritan' were inspired by the dramatic scenery, and in this case, the hazardous road between Jericho and Jerusalem (Luke 10:30).

Jericho stands as testimony to the power of faith. Trusting in God may indeed see walls brought down (Hebrews 11:30); sight received (Mark 10:52); prejudice overcome (Luke 10:30–33); human nature transformed (Luke 19:8); and salvation experienced (Luke 19:9-10).

VIEW OVER JERICHO

VIEW
OVER
JERICHO

The Walls of Jerusalem

The sacrifices of God are a broken spirit; a broken and contrite heart, O God, you will not despise. In your good pleasure make Zion prosper; build up the walls of Jerusalem. (Psalm 51:17–18)

DAMASCUS GATE, JERUSALEM

TORAH SCROLL, WESTERN WALL, JERUSALEM

The ancient city of Jerusalem is situated on a spur of land where three deep wadis, the Kidron, Tyropoean and Hinnom, merge to form one valley sloping south towards the Dead Sea. Jerusalem was first settled by the Amorites and Hittites (Ezekiel 16:3,45).

Indeed the name 'Jerusalem' means 'founded by the god Shalem' after one of the Amorite gods. Jerusalem's long history is written in its walls as they were built up, seiged, demolished, rebuilt and expanded by its successive inhabitants; so much so that Jerusalem has been the scene of conflict on over 40 occasions during its history.

The earliest walls of ancient settlements were often made of earth or clay bricks mixed with reed. Over time these were vulnerable to erosion from the weather, structural instability of destruction by fire. For this reason they are often difficult to locate or date with certainty (Isaiah 30:13; Amos 1:7,10,14). The earliest known walls of Jerusalem were made of stone and exploited the natural defensible terrain to the east, south and west (Isaiah 2:15; 9:10; Zephaniah 1:16).

Although mentioned in the demarcation of the land taken by Judah and Benjamin (Joshua 18:15), Jerusalem first gained significance to the Israelites when David captured the Jebusite city and made it his capital. He may have done so because it was more central than Hebron to the emerging kingdom formed from the twelve tribes of Israel. David made use of the Jebusite fortifications which may have included only one gate (2 Samuel 15:2). Solomon was probably the first to incorporate the northern hill of Mount Moriah within the city walls having built the temple there around 1010 BC. In 722 BC, with the fall of the northern kingdom, refugees arrived in Jerusalem and Hezekiah enlarged the walls to the west to

OLD CITY WALLS AND CITADEL, JERUSALEM

contain the burgeoning population. These walls were sufficiently impregnable to survive the siege of Sennacherib in 702 BC, and traces remain today (2 Chronicles 32:5). Nebuchadnezzar, the king of Babylon, destroyed the city in 586 BC following a siege that lasted three years (2 Kings 25; Jeremiah 39). The temple and palaces were destroyed by fire and the walls again razed to the ground. These were rebuilt under Ezra and Nehemiah in around 430 BC, following the return of some of the Israelites from exile in Babylon (Nehemiah 2–3). Nehemiah's description of the walls and gates of Jerusalem is the most comprehensive to be found anywhere in the Bible. It is likely that use was made of the existing foundations and that the gates were given their former names (Nehemiah 12:31–39).

Josephus, the Jewish historian, provides us with the most detailed record of the walls of the first century AD in his book *The Jewish Wars*. He specifically mentions three walls which incorporated the work of Solomon, Hezekiah, Nehemiah, the Hasmoneans and Herod the Great. Remains of a wall and tower dated to the seventh century BC have been found under the Roman Cardo which are four metres thick and eight metres high. Another discovery known as the Broad Wall, dated to the work of Hezekiah in the eighth century BC, is seven metres wide.

With the capture of Jerusalem by the Romans, the city witnessed significant changes to its shape and size. In AD 41, for instance, Herod Agrippa doubled the size of the city by building a third wall on the north and west sides of the city which also, incidentally, brought the site of Calvary inside the wall. This was, however, never completed, as the entire city was destroyed in AD 70 by the Romans. Hadrian

LION GATE, JERUSALEM

eventually rebuilt it, including its walls, renaming in Colonia Aelia Capitolina. His work included the enlargement of the northern wall which became 6 metres wide and 13 metres high with 90 towers. The walls of Jerusalem today, with their 35 towers and eight gates, are largely the work of Suleiman the Magnificent and date from the sixteenth century. In places they are built over a patchwork of much earlier walls and gates and the immense layers of rubble accumulated over thousands of years.

In the Bible, walls are used to symbolise many things but especially to describe salvation. It is good to remember that our security should never rest in stone defences but in God alone who is our eternal rock (Isaiah 26:1; 60:18). So often walls are built to exclude or divide people. Jesus Christ has broken down the wall of separation between Jew and Gentile that had once existed in the temple, enabling all people to come to know God through him. It is for us to live out this equal grace and common justice in our divided world (Ephesians 2:14).

The Mount of Olives

When he came near the place where the road goes down the Mount of Olives, the whole crowd of disciples began joyfully to praise God in loud voices for all the miracles they had seen:'Blessed is the king who comes in the name of the Lord!'Peace in heaven and glory in the highest!' (Luke 19:37–38)

The Mount of Olives is actually a ridge of hills running from north to south for about 4 kilometres to the east of Jerusalem and parallel to the deep ravine of the Kidron Valley. As the name suggests, the hillsides were once covered with dense olive groves. To the east lie the villages of Bethphage and Bethany and beyond them, the Judean wilderness and the Jordan Valley. The barren hills of Moab and the Dead Sea are also visible from this strategic vantage point. For this reason it was known as Jerusalem's watchtower.

The northern end became known as Mount Scopus, meaning 'lookout' because the Roman general Titus used it for his headquarters during the fateful siege of Jerusalem in AD 70. Until the time of Christ, the Mount of Olives had been heavily wooded with many olive trees. These were, however, cut down and used for battering rams and siege machines by the Romans when they destroyed the city.

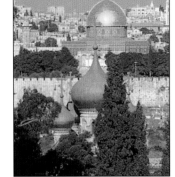

OLD CITY FROM THE
MOUNT OF OLIVES

MOUNT OF OLIVES, JERUSALEM

At the southern end where the Kidron Valley merges with the Valley of Hinnom it is called the Mount of Corruption. Here, where previously the Israelites had worshipped God (2 Samuel 15:30–32), and may have fulfilled the purification ceremony of the red heifer (Numbers 19), King Solomon built 'high places' for *'Ashtoreth the vile goddess of the Sidonians, for Chemosh the vile god of Moab, and for Molech the detestable god of the people of Ammon'* (2 Kings 23:13). These were

OLD OLIVE TREE,
MOUNT OF OLIVES

later desecrated by King Josiah who covered the sites with human bones and cut down the Asherah poles to purify the religious practices of Israel (2 Chronicles 34:1–7). Subsequently, the Mount of Olives became associated with the departure of the *shekinah* glory of God from the temple as a sign of Israel's impending exile (Ezekiel 10:18; 11:23).

Parallels between Old and New Testament events which occurred on the Mount of Olives are significant. In the time of Nehemiah, for example, following their return from captivity in Babylon, the Israelites probably gathered branches from the olive trees here, as well as palm branches, to make booths to celebrate the Feast of Tabernacles (Nehemiah 8:15). On what became known as Palm Sunday, the disciples of Jesus similarly gathered branches from the Mount of Olives with which to greet their king as he entered Jerusalem.

Jesus was not the first king of Israel to weep over Jerusalem from the Mount of Olives. When Absalom rebelled against his father David, the deposed king fled the city, his feet bare and head covered in shame. As he looked back over Jerusalem from the Mount of Olives he wept (2 Samuel 15:30–32), even acknowledging that Shimei's curse on him may have been from God (2 Samuel 16:5–10). Centuries later the Lord Jesus wept over Jerusalem from this spot knowing that within days they would call for his crucifixion, rejecting God's way of peace and reconciliation. Jesus would willingly have been cursed in their place but they refused. In tears, Jesus foretold the consequent destruction of Jerusalem as the result of God's judgement upon Israel (Luke 19:41–44).

During the last week of his life Jesus spent much time with his disciples on the Mount of Olives (Mark 13:3–37; Luke 21:37; 22:39). With its dense foliage and cool evening breezes perhaps it reminded him of Galilee, providing a welcome retreat from the tension of the overcrowded city. Repudiating their mistaken belief that he was still going to restore a physical kingdom to Israel, Jesus commanded them instead to leave Jerusalem and become his witnesses taking the gospel to the whole world. From the Mount of Olives, the Lord physically ascended to heaven, angels promising he would return in the same way (Acts 1:6–12). Zechariah had previously predicted this, indicating that when the Lord Jesus Christ returns to judge the earth, it will be to the Mount of Olives. This dramatic event will be marked by a radical change to its topography. '*On that day his feet will stand on the Mount of Olives, east of Jerusalem, and the Mount of Olives will be split in two from east to west, forming a great valley, with half of the mountain moving north and half moving south*' (Zechariah 14:4).

It's easy to be a Christian on Palm Sunday when the sun is shining and we are surrounded by many others worshipping the Lord. It is not so easy on Maundy Thursday when it is dark, we are alone or the future uncertain. Then it is time to remember that it is but a short distance from the Mount of Olives to the Garden of Gethsemane. Before being a place of resurrection and ascension it was first a place of denial and rejection. Ironically the word 'witness' comes from the same word as 'martyr'. For many Christians to be a witness for Christ literally means being a martyr also. Jesus calls us to both (Mark 8:34–38; Acts 1:8–9) and to identify with Paul when he said '*For to me, to live is Christ and to die is gain*' (Philippians 1:21).

MOUNT OF OLIVES, JERUSALEM

The Garden of Gethsemane

They went to a place called Gethsemane, and Jesus said to his disciples, 'Sit here while I pray'. He took Peter, James and John along with him, and began to be deeply distressed and troubled. 'My soul is overwhelmed with sorrow to the point of death,' he said to them. 'Stay here and keep watch.' Going a little further, he fell to the ground and prayed that if possible the hour might pass from him. 'Abba, Father,' he said, 'everything is possible for you. Take this cup from me. Yet not what I will, but what you will.' (Mark 14:32–36)

OLIVE TREES
AT GETHSEMANE

Gethsemane means 'oil press' in Aramaic and is situated on the Mount of Olives across the Kidron Valley and overlooking the temple of Jerusalem. The various references in the Gospels suggest that this was an enclosed piece of ground which Jesus 'entered' (Matthew 26:36). John very specifically mentions that it was a garden (John 18:1). The exact location is not known since in AD 70 Titus cut down all the trees on the Mount of Olives in his siege of Jerusalem.

OLIVE TREE TRUNK

Jesus came to the Garden of Gethsemane often to pray alone and to be with his disciples, especially in the evenings leading up to his trial and crucifixion. This may indeed have been the place where he lodged when visiting Jerusalem (Luke 21:37; 22:39). After sharing the Last Supper with his disciples Jesus took them to the Garden of Gethsemane one last time to pray in preparation for his imminent betrayal and arrest (Matthew 26:36–46). Judas, knowing this was where Jesus would be, brought the Jewish religious leaders to arrest him in the Garden (Matthew 26:47–56).

The Bordeaux Pilgrim writing in AD 333 specifically mentions the existence of a vineyard with a rock where Judas betrayed Jesus.

Satan. He was overcome with sorrow knowing what lay before him, yet he submitted obediently to the will of God, 'My Father, if it is not possible for this cup to be taken away unless I drink it, may your will be done' (Matthew 26:38; 42). He was tempted as we are, yet withstood the test and overcame (Hebrews 5:7–9). Therefore we can identify with him as he has done with us. 'Let us fix our eyes on Jesus, the author and perfecter of our faith, who for the joy set before him endured the cross, scorning its shame, and sat down at the right

The first church to commemorate the events of the Garden of Gethsemane at the foot of the Mount of Olives was probably built by Theodosius between AD 379-384. This was destroyed by the Persians and rebuilt by the Crusaders. Today the Church of All Nations, completed in 1924, stands on the site over the 'rock of agony' on which it is believed Jesus prayed before his arrest. Beside the church is a simple but beautiful garden with eight very old olive trees, the largest of which has a girth of nearly six metres. Olive trees never die so it is possible the trees that survive today have grown from the stumps of those that witnessed the sad events that first Maundy Thursday. Carbon-dating tests carried out in 1982 confirm that some of the wood may be 2,300 years old.

It was in the Garden of Gethsemane, alone, just as in the Judean wilderness at the beginning of his ministry, that Jesus was tempted by

hand of the throne of God. Consider him who endured such opposition from sinful men, so that you will not grow weary and lose heart' (Hebrews 12:2–3).

It is possible that the apostles say there is a parallel with the Garden of Eden where the first Adam disobeyed God and sin and death entered the world. Here in another garden the second Adam overcame temptation and by his death in our place brought forgiveness and life (Romans 5:15–17; 1 Corinthians 15:21–22).

If you ever find yourself too tired to pray, or perhaps in dark times have felt unable to pray or been tempted to deny Christ, remember the events in the Garden of Gethsemane. The apostles have been there before you. Like Peter, take a few moments to confess your sin, recommit yourself to follow Christ and hear his words of comfort and love (John 21:15–17; 1 John 1:8–10).

OLIVE TREE,
ISRAEL

88

Jerusalem from St Peter in Galicantu

'O Jerusalem, Jerusalem, you who kill the prophets and stone those sent to you, how often I have longed to gather your children together, as a hen gathers her chicks under her wings, but you were not willing. Look, your house is left to you desolate. For I tell you, you will not see me again until you say, "Blessed is he who comes in the name of the Lord."' (Matthew 23:37–39)

The panoramic view of Jerusalem from St Peter in Galicantu is simply stunning. To the left is Mount Zion, traditional site of David's tomb, the Upper Room and the Last Supper. Dominating the view, however, is the south face of the Temple Mount. The enormity of the foundations for this structure are staggering, covering an area of about 35 acres, 446 metres from north to south and 296 metres from east to west. The recently excavated first-century temple steps and bricked-up archway entrance used by Jesus are still visible today. At the south-east corner, originally 45 metres high above the Kidron Valley, stands what many regard as the pinnacle of the temple from where Satan tempted Jesus to throw himself down (Matthew 4:5–7). Behind the temple area, providing a rich green backdrop of olive trees, lies the Kidron Valley and the Mount of Olives. To the right and lower down, are the excavations of David's City, the Pool of Siloam and the Valley of Gehenna which joins the Kidron Valley before beginning its slow, winding descent to the Dead Sea.

The site first gained significance as Mount Moriah because it was here that Abraham was tested over

18TH–CENTURY STEPS BY ST PETER

CHURCH OF ST PETER IN GALICANTU PROBABLY BUILT OVER THE HOUSE OF CAIAPHAS

ST PETER IN GALICANTU

the sacrifice of Isaac (2 Chronicles 3:1; Genesis 22:1–14). David acquired the hill from Araunah the Jebusite in order to offer a sacrifice to God and save his people (2 Samuel 24:16–25). The privilege of building the temple, however, was given to his son Solomon (1 Kings 5). The remains of the temple walls seen today are actually the third to be built on the site. The first was constructed by Solomon, followed by Zerubbabel, and then Herod. These represent the pre-exilic, post-exilic, and New Testament periods.

The proximity and juxtaposition of the Temple Mount to the Valley of Gehenna is both sobering and profound. *Gehenna* is the Greek for Hinnon and means the 'valley of whining' or 'lamentation'. In the Old Testament it is the place where children were sacrificed to the pagan deities of Baal and Molech (2 Kings 16:3; 17:17; 23:10). Not surprisingly, perhaps, Jesus used the same emotive place to illustrate the eternal reality of hell (Matthew 5:22, 29; 23:15).

The splendid view of Jerusalem from this hilltop encompasses most of the events which occurred in Holy Week. The Last Supper was probably held in the Essene Quarter on what is now Mount Zion, since the disciples were told to follow a man carrying a water pot (Mark 14:13–16). As dusk fell that Maundy Thursday Jesus walked with his disciples over to the Garden of Gethsemane on the Mount of Olives to pray (Luke 22:39–46). There he was arrested by the Jewish religious leaders and brought to the House of Caiaphas for interrogation overnight (Luke 22:47–54). Early on Good Friday he was taken to Pilate, probably in the Antonia Fortress at the north-west corner of the Temple Mount (Luke 23:1–2). After his trial Jesus was led along what is now known as the Via Dolorosa carrying his cross to the place of crucifixion which was then outside the city walls (Matthew 27:27–33). After his death our Lord was placed in a new tomb in a garden nearby (Matthew 27:57–66). Three momentous days later the risen Lord met with the disciples in the Upper Room again before ascending to heaven before their very eyes from the Mount of Olives (John 20:19–31). It is to this same spot that many believe he will return (Acts 1:9–11). This explains the presence of extensive Jewish, Muslim and Christian cemeteries on the slopes of the Kidron Valley and Mount of Olives as all three faiths believe the dead will rise first when the Messiah comes.

This scene then is one of stark contrasts. Calvary, the Mount of Olives and Gehenna. We see in one panoramic view locations associated with both the way to heaven and the path to hell. It is a scene that sums up the heart of our historic credal statements as well as the personal choice before us all. *'See, I set before you today life and prosperity, death and destruction. For I command you today to love the LORD your God, to walk in his ways, and to keep his commands, decrees and laws; then you will live and increase, and the LORD your God will bless you ... This day I call heaven and earth as witnesses against you that I have set before you life and death, blessings and curses. Now choose life, so that you and your children may live and that you may love the LORD your God, listen to his voice, and hold fast to him'* (Deuteronomy 30:15–16, 19–20).

JERUSALEM
SEEN FROM
ST PETER
IN
GALICANTU

93

Golgotha

At the place where Jesus was crucified, there was a garden, and in the garden a new tomb, in which no – one had ever been laid. Because it was the Jewish day of Preparation and since the tomb was near by, they laid Jesus there. (John 19:41–42)

There are two places associated with Calvary in Jerusalem today. The traditional site has been venerated since before Hadrian (AD 117-138) built a pagan shrine to Venus over the tomb and a statue to Jupiter on Golgotha to eliminate the Christian churches.

THE ROCKY OUTCROP RESEMBLING A SKULL WHICH CAUGHT THE EYE OF GENERAL GORDON

In AD 326, Queen Helena, the mother of the emperor Constantine was shown the site by Bishop Macarius, and had the pagan temple demolished. In its place she built the Church of the Holy Sepulchre to encompass both the site of Calvary and the tomb of Jesus.

The other location, north of the Damascus Gate, has been venerated since 1885 when the rather eccentric General Charles Gordon popularised the notion that a rocky hill at the back of a disused quarry appeared to match the skull-like description of Calvary. One of its names, Betha-Sekilah, means 'Place of Stoning'. Its proximity to a tomb discovered in 1849 seemed to corroborate this assertion. The tomb itself may date from the time of Herod Agrippa (AD 37–44), although the doorway and windows appear to be Byzantine or later. Gordon disputed the authenticity of the Church of the Holy Sepulchre because it lies within the walls of Jerusalem. Jews would not bury their dead within a populated area because tombs were regarded as unclean. What Gordon did not appreciate, however, was that the Ottoman walls of the sixteenth century were built further north than those of the first-century Roman Jerusalem so, later, encompassing the area around the Church of the Holy Sepulchre. Evangelical tastes also came to prefer the simplicity of the Garden Tomb to the ornate and complex oriental religious shrines

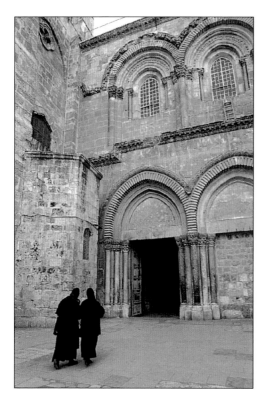

CHURCH OF THE HOLY SEPULCHRE, JERUSALEM

within the Church of the Holy Sepulchre.

Scriptures give us some clues as to the location of Calvary.

Matthew, Luke and John specifically mention that this was a new tomb in which no one had yet been buried, one that was sealed with a rolling stone (Matthew 27:59–60; Luke 23:50–53; John 19:41). John and the writer of Hebrews emphasise that Jesus was crucified outside the city walls (John 19:20; Hebrews 13:12) while John specifically mentions that the tomb was within a garden (John 19:41). Matthew adds that Jesus was buried in a tomb belonging to Joseph of Arimathea, a wealthy member of the Sanhedrin who had not consented to the execution of Jesus but was himself a secret disciple (Matthew 27:57–60).

The place where Christ was crucified is called Golgotha in the Gospels. This is the transliteration of an Aramaic word meaning 'the place of the skull' (Mark 15:22). The word is also used twice in the Old Testament, literally of the skulls of Abimelech and Jezebel (Judges 9:53; 2 Kings 9:35). Our English word 'Calvary' means the same thing and comes from the Latin 'calvaria'. It is probable that the location was given this name because it was a place of execution and a skull symbolised death.

In ancient Palestine, caves were commonly used as graves or tombs. Over several generations, members of the same family would share a cave to bury their deceased. The word 'sepulchre' is translated from the Hebrew and refers to a niche that was carved out of the side of the cave in which the body of a deceased person would be placed (Genesis 23:6). When only the bones remained they would be gathered and placed at the back of the cave, sometimes in a sarcophagus. Jewish tombs had small niches carved out of the walls in which bodies were placed. First-century examples of these can still be seen at the back of the Syrian chapel within the Church of the Resurrection, ironically named the Tomb of Joseph of Arimathea.

The most significant fact about the tomb of Jesus, however, is not its exact geographical location. What matters is that it was empty. 'He is not here; he risen!' (Luke 24:6). Only after they had encountered the risen Lord did the disciples begin to comprehend his incredible promise, 'I am the resurrection and the life. He who believes in me will live, even though he dies; and whoever lives and believes in me will never die' (John 11:25–26). At Golgotha, heaven and earth unite, where time and eternity meet. The place uniquely demonstrates to us the extent of God's unconditional love, the cost of achieving forgiveness for our sin, and proclaims the assurance of life everlasting. Have you acknowledged that Jesus died in your place in order that you may share his risen life (1 Peter 3:18; Romans 5:8)?

INTERIOR OF GARDEN TOMB (POSSIBLE BURIAL SITE OF JESUS), JERUSALEM

ROCK FACE (SKULL), POSSIBLE GOLGOTHA SITE, JERUSALEM

The Western Wall

O God, the nations have invaded your inheritance; they have defiled your holy temple, they have reduced Jerusalem to rubble ... We are objects of reproach to our neighbours, of scorn and derision to those around us. How long, O LORD? Will you be angry for ever? How long will your jealousy burn like fire? (Psalm 79:1, 4–5)

David's lament has epitomised the deep feelings and aspirations of Jews down the centuries who have come to the Western or 'Wailing' Wall to pray (Psalm 79:1,4–5). When the temple was destroyed in July AD 70 the Western Wall became the focus of Jewish religious life in Jerusalem. The Hebrew prophets themselves gave an answer to this lament, although their message has not always been welcomed or heeded. *'Rend your heart and not your garments. Return to the LORD your God, for he is gracious and compassionate, slow to anger and abounding in love, and he relents from sending calamity. Who knows? He may turn and have pity and leave behind a blessing...'* (Joel 2:13–14).

The lowest seven courses of stone visible in the Western Wall date back to the Jewish temple built by Herod the Great between 18 BC and AD 28. Below the pavement level a further nineteen courses reach a depth of 21 metres. Some of these stones which make up the retaining wall of the Temple Mount measure more than 12 metres in length and one is known to weigh 400 tons. The temple walls were constructed so precisely that there was no need for mortar or cement, the stones simply resting one on top of the other. The entire Western Wall of the Temple Mount is 485 metres long although only 57 metres is accessible today. Above the Herodian foundations, the stone work is made up of progressively smaller and smaller stones which date back to the Roman, Muslim and Ottoman periods.

It is possible that the open area adjacent to the Wall today was at the time of Christ an open porticoed plaza used for public gatherings, described by Josephus as the Xystos. It lies on top of some 21 metres of

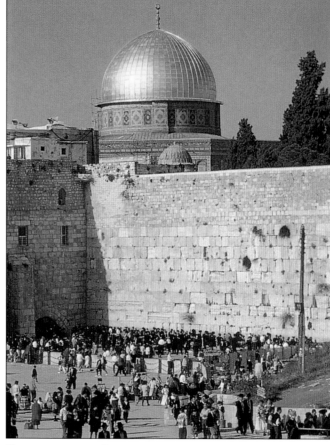

DOME OF THE ROCK, JERUSALEM

WESTERN WALL, JERUSALEM

debris built up during the Hellenistic and Roman periods filling in and levelling what was once the Tyropoean Valley. Archaeology has also revealed that this area was previously the site of a Hellenistic gymnasium built by Jason (2 Maccabees 4:12). Even earlier burial remains discovered here indicate that this area was outside Solomon's walls in the eighth century BC, before the city expanded west.

Jews were prohibited from entering Jerusalem following the destruction of the city in AD 70 and it was not until sometime after the death of Hadrian in 138 that they were allowed to return annually on the 9th July to lament the destruction of the temple. Gradually, as the prohibition was relaxed, Jews began to settle in Jerusalem in small numbers and came to pray near the Temple Mount on other occasions. With the capture of Jerusalem by the Muslims and the construction of shrines on the Temple Mount area, Jews were again denied access and the Western Wall became the nearest location for pilgrimage. For many centuries Jews came here to pray, especially on Friday evenings at the beginning of their Sabbath, to lament the downfall of Jerusalem and the temple. In 1930 the League of Nations declared the area around the Western Wall, known as the Moors' Quarter, to be a Muslim holy place, although the narrow alley adjacent to the Wall remained accessible to Jews for prayer. However, when Israel occupied the city in 1967 they demolished Arab homes and mosques next to the Wall to create the wide plaza now utilised by Jews as a synagogue for

A TORAH AT THE WESTERN WALL

prayer, celebrations and bar mitzvah ceremonies.

Today, the Western Wall is a vivid reminder that God no longer dwells in temples made by hands (Acts 17:24). Jesus fulfilled and annulled the role of the temple in the purposes of God. Jesus cleansed the temple which was originally intended to be for all nations (John 2:13–17; Malachi 3:1). He also predicted its destruction because the Jews rejected their Messiah (Matthew 23:37–24:2). Jesus taught that he himself was greater than the temple (Matthew 12:6) and when his authority was questioned, described his body as the temple that mattered (John 2:19). Jesus also taught that the Church would be the new eschatological temple (Matthew 18:19–20; John 14:23) a theme developed by the apostles (1 Corinthians 3:16; 6:19; 2 Corinthians 6:16). By his death Jesus has opened a new way into the presence of God making the Jewish temple unnecessary, a mere fading shadow of the true reality in heaven (Ephesians 2:14–22; Hebrews 8:1–10:18). The New Jerusalem which will one day come down from heaven needs no temple, for we shall see God face to face (Revelation 21:22; 22:4). God's answer therefore to those who still seek him at the Western Wall or even a rebuilt temple may be summarised in Jesus' reply to the Samaritan woman, '*Believe me, woman, a time is coming when you will worship the Father neither on this mountain nor in Jerusalem . . . Yet a time is coming and has now come when the true worshippers will worship the Father in spirit and truth, for they are the kind of worshippers the Father seeks. God is spirit, and his worshippers must worship in spirit and in truth*'(John 4:21–24).

A South-Western
View of The
Tempie Mount

Joppa

In Joppa there was a disciple named Tabitha (which, when translated, is Dorcas), who was always doing good and helping the poor. (Acts 9:36)

Joppa, also called Jaffa today, means 'beauty' in Hebrew. It is indeed a beautiful as well as strategic location, set on a rocky outcrop on the Mediterranean coast, the only natural harbour between Egypt and Akko. For this reason it was prized by the Pharaoh Thutmose III (c. 1468 BC) as well as Ramases II (c. 1304–1237). In the Amarna letters, for example, the beauty of its gardens are noted as well as the skill of its workers in leather and wood. It is first mentioned in the Bible as part of the inheritance of the Tribe of Dan (Joshua 19:46), although it largely

THE WATERFRONT OF THE OLD TOWN OF JOPPA

remained a Philistine stronghold until King David captured it. In the second century BC, conflict between the Maccabees and Greek residents led to its destruction by fire in 142 BC (2 Maccabees 12:3–8). Only then did it become an Israelite town. Pompey captured the town in 63 BC and Antony gave it to Cleopatra of Egypt.

Joppa began to lose its influence as a port when in 22 BC Herod began construction of Caesarea to the north. Joppa had always been a difficult harbour to navigate because of the reefs which form a breakwater about 100 metres off shore. Until the rise of air travel, Joppa remained the main port through which pilgrims passed on their way to the Holy Land.

Joppa is mentioned several times in the Bible. It was to Joppa that

FISHING BOATS IN JOPPA HARBOUR

rafts of cedarwood from Lebanon were brought for transport overland to Jerusalem for King Solomon to construct the first temple (2 Chronicles 2:16). The same route was used for transporting wood for the second temple commissioned by Cyrus (Ezra 3:7).

Joppa features again in the story of Jonah as the Phoenician port from which the prophet tried to evade the Lord's commission to preach in the wicked city of Nineveh, later the capital of the Assyrian empire (Jonah 1:3). Jonah had probably grown up to hate the Assyrians and their evil practices (Nahum 3:1–19). His antipathy was so strong that he did not want them to hear of God's mercy (Jonah 4:2–3) even though this had always been God's purpose and Israel's mission (Genesis 12:3; Isaiah 42:6).

In the New Testament, it was also coincidentally in Joppa that the apostle Peter appeared to show a similar reluctance to recognise God's compassion for the Gentiles. Here Peter received a rather less drastic lesson through a vision of various kinds of clean and unclean good (Acts 10:9–16). Peter's vision prepared him to receive the servants of Cornelius who were already on their way from Caesarea to take him back to explain the gospel to the Gentiles. It is interesting that Peter had already chosen to stay in the home of Simon the tanner in Joppa, since by associating with someone who handled the skins of dead animals he was unclean according to Jewish law. Perhaps Peter's willingness to reject such prejudice helped prepare him for this vision of an inclusive gospel and the realisation that 'God does not show favouritism but accepts men from every nation who fear him and do what is right' (Acts 10:34–35). When the Holy Spirit came upon them in the same way as he had done in Jerusalem on the Day of Pentecost, Peter and the other Jewish believers could no longer view the Gentiles as inferior people excluded from God's saving grace.

Joppa reminds us then of a double lesson: it is futile to run away from God's will, and the proclamation of the good news of Jesus Christ to all people must always be our first priority. We were no more deserving that anyone else, for we are all sinners saved by grace (1 Timothy 2:3–6). This is why there is no place for any distinctions based on race within the Church for, 'There is neither Jew nor Greek, slave nor free, male nor female, for you are all one in Christ Jesus (Galatians 3:28).

ST PETER'S CHURCH

HARBOUR
FRONT,
JAFFA

Caesarea

Then Peter began to speak: 'I now realise how true it is that God does not show favouritism but accepts men from every nation who fear him and do what is right.' (Acts 10:34–35)

ROMAN THEATRE, CAESAREA

Caesarea is on the Mediterranean coast between the ancient cities of Jaffa and Dor, on the main coastal road between Tyre and Egypt. Because of the lack of any natural harbour between Sidon and Egypt, the Sidonian king Abdashtart built a fortified anchorage in the fourth century BC. It was called Strabo's Tower after the Greek translation of his name. It became a Greek settlement from 332 BC when Alexander the Great conquered Palestine. During what was a turbulent period it was controlled briefly by the Hasmonean ruler Alexander Jannaeus from 96 BC before Pompey took it in 63 BC. It was then given to Cleopatra by Mark Antony, but when Octavian Augustus won the battle of Actium in 30 BC he gave the town as a gift to Herod the Great.

Herod took twelve years between 25 and 13 BC to build a magnificent new capital city and harbour based on Hellenistic architecture. He built palaces, a hippodrome, a theatre, an amphitheatre overlooking the sea, a sewer system and an aqueduct which brought water from Mount Carmel. The harbour was a massive engineering project protected by two long semicircular breakwaters 65 metres wide to the north and south of the entrance. These were constructed with giant mortared stones each more than 15 metres long, 5 metres wide and nearly 3 metres deep, which were sunk to a depth of twenty fathoms. Giant statues were erected at the entrance depicting Augustus and Roma. An inner harbour was dug into the shore to enable ships to berth next to vaulted warehouses.

Herod renamed the city Caesarea Maritima since his patron had become Caesar Augustus. The port itself was named Limen Sebastos. Caesarea was the capital of the Roman province of Judea for over 600 years. It was also the headquarters for the Roman army occupying Palestine. It was in Caesarea that King Herod Agrippa I, grandson of Herod the Great, was struck down by an angel for accepting the acclaim of the people that he was divine (Acts 12:19–23). It may also

ROMAN AQUEDUCT, CAESAREA

ROMAN AQUEDUCT AT SUNSET, CAESAREA

have been divine retribution for executing James, the brother of the apostle John, and for persecuting the Church (Acts 12:1–18).

Caesarea was the strategic focal point in Palestine for the spread of the gospel to the Gentile world. It is remembered as the place where God led a reluctant Peter to share the good news of Jesus Christ with the Roman centurion Cornelius and his family. They became the first Gentiles to believe and be baptised in the name of Jesus Christ (Acts 10:1–8; 22–48). Philip the evangelist, who led the Ethiopian eunuch to Christ, also lived in Caesarea with his four daughters (Acts 8:26–40; 21:8–9).

Paul used the port of Caesarea to escape to Tarsus after threats were made to kill him in Jerusalem (Acts 9:30). He also landed at Caesarea after both his second and third missionary journeys (Acts 18:22; 21:8). Later, Paul was held as a prisoner in Caesarea for two years (Acts 23:31–26:32). There, while on trial, God gave Paul the opportunity to make his defence of the Christian faith before the Roman governor Antonius Felix (Acts 24:1–26); his successor, Porcius Festus (Acts 25:1–22); and also King Herod Agrippa II (Acts 25:23–26:32). From Caesarea Paul was eventually taken to Rome having appealed to be tried before Caesar.

The history of Christian witness in Caesarea teaches us that God can use opposition, persecution and even the imprisonment of his servants to spread the gospel. We must not be discouraged by adversity or intimidated by hostility. The gospel cannot be chained or silenced. The blood of the martyrs is indeed the seed of the Church.

THE REMAINS OF THE CRUSADER CITADEL AND HARBOUR, CAESAREA

Pisidian Antioch

From Perga they went on to Pisidian Antioch. On the Sabbath they entered the synagogue and sat down. After the reading from the Law and the Prophets, the synagogue rulers sent word to them, saying, 'Brothers, if you have a message of encouragement for the people, please speak.'... As Paul and Barnabas were leaving the synagogue, the people invited them to speak further about these things on the next Sabbath. When the congregation was dismissed, many of the Jews and devout converts to Judaism followed Paul and Barnabas, who talked with them and urged them to continue in the grace of God. On the next Sabbath almost the whole city gathered to hear the word of the Lord. (Acts 13:14–15, 42–44)

Pisidian Antioch was founded by the Seleucid king, Seleucus I Nicator around 300 BC. The site is on a plateau close to the west bank of the River Athios, on the edge of the Pisidian Mountains, to the north of Pamphylia and the Taurus Mountains, east of Phrygia and to the west of Lycaonia and Cilicia. The River Athios flows from the Sultan Dagh to the double lake called Egerdir Gol and the area around Pisidian Antioch is very fertile. The city was named after Nicator's father, Antiochus, as were many others, such as Phrygian Antioch and the Seleucid capital of Antioch in Syria (Acts 13:1–3).

The Seleucids chose strategic sites such as Pisidian Antioch to control the local tribes and to exploit the great trade route between the Cilician Gates and Ephesus. Xenophon describes how the indigenous people of Pisidia were independent of the kings of Persia from the fifth century BC and that even Alexander the Great had difficulty subjugating these warlike people.

In 189 BC, the Romans declared Pisidian Antioch a 'free city', its citizens no longer were required to pay tribute to the Seleucid kings. In 39 BC, Antony gave the city to Amyntas of Galatia and so Pisidian Antioch was transferred to the province of Galatia. The city was made a Roman colony in 6 BC and renamed Caesarea Antiocheia. It became the administrative capital of the province of Galatia and the

ROMAN AQUEDUCT AT PSIDIAN ANTIOCH

THE THEATRE

aroused the hostility of the local Jews, threatened by Gentiles coming to faith (Acts 13:48–51). In the region of Pisidia and Phrygia women held positions of wealth and civic office, such as magistrates, and Paul's enemies exploited some of them to ensure he was expelled, but not for long (Acts 13:50). It is likely that this area held a special place in Paul's heart, as his friend and disciple Timothy was from nearby Lystra (Acts 16:1).

Paul visited Psidian Antioch on each of his missionary journeys (Acts 14:21; 16:6; 18:23) and it is quite possible that it was in this wild and rugged area of Pisidia that he encountered what he describes as, 'danger from bandits . . .' and, 'danger in the country . . .' (Acts 14:21–25; 2 Corinthians 11:26).

Pisidian Antioch reminds us that while the human spirit cannot be tamed by external military force but only by Jesus Christ, '. . . everyone who wants to live a godly life in Christ Jesus will be persecuted' (2 Timothy 3:12).

most important Roman garrison colony in Asia. Augustus took steps to pacify Pisidia even further by building a network of roads from Pisidian Antioch to five other military colonies at Cremna, Comama, Oblasa, Parlais and Lystra, the latter being called the Royal Road. An inscription has been discovered showing that Quirinius who was governor of Syria at the time of the birth of Christ (Luke 2:2), was also an honorary magistrate of the colony at Pisidian Antioch.

From here the Romans attempted, like the Selucids, to subjugate the rebellious tribes of Pisidia, Isauria and Pamphylia. They imposed Latin as the official language although the discovery of Phrygian inscriptions indicates the cosmopolitan nature of the local population.

It is easy to see why Paul used Psidian Antioch as his base for reaching the region of southern Galatia (Acts 13:49), at least until he

BYZANTINE CHURCH

Pergamum

'To the angel of the church in Pergamum write: These are the words of him who has the sharp, double-edged sword. I know where you live – where Satan has his throne. Yet you remain true to my name. You did not renounce your faith in me, even in the days of Antipas, my faithful witness, who was put to death in your city – where Satan lives. Nevertheless, I have a few things against you: You have people there who hold to the teaching of Balaam, who taught Balak to entice the Israelites to sin by eating food sacrificed to idols and by committing sexual immorality. Likewise you also have those who hold to the teaching of the Nicolaitans. Repent therefore! Otherwise, I will soon come to you and will fight against them with the sword of my mouth. He who has an ear, let him hear what the Spirit says to the churches.' (Revelation 2:12–17)

THE ASCLEPION, PERGAMUM

Pergamum is situated on a commanding hill in the Caicus Valley, about five kilometres from the Caicus River, opposite the island of Lesbos, about twenty-four kilometres from the Aegean Sea in north-west Turkey. Although the settlement is known to have been founded well before the fourth century BC, Pergamum rose in prominence after 282 BC when Philetaerus rebelled against Thrace and made it the capital of the emerging Attalid kingdom in the region of Mysia.

Pergamum came to be seen as a symbol of Greek supremacy over the Barbarians. Besides many fine buildings, the library in Pergamum, for example, grew in size and prestige until it contained over 200,000 volumes and rivalled that of Alexandria. Because of this the Egyptians banned exports of papyrus to Pergamum. Scholars there devised a new material for writing known as *Pergamena charta*, or parchment, named after the city.

THE TEMPLE OF TRAJAN, PERGAMUM

In 133 BC, Attalus III bequeathed the city to the Romans and it became the capital of their province of Asia. Ironically Mark Antony gave Pergamum's library to Cleopatra as a sign of their friendship and its priceless volumes were moved to Alexandria.

The city was also a focus for the worship of four important Greek gods: Zeus, Athena, Dionysus and Aesclepius. Aesclepius was the pagan god of healing and archaeologists have found the hospital complex where sick people from the surrounding region were brought in the hope of finding a cure here.

Pergamum is the third city of the 'seven churches of Asia' mentioned in the book of Revelation which reflects its geographical position after Ephesus and Smyrna (Revelation 1:11). Pergamum is described as the place, 'where Satan has his throne' (Revelation 2:13). This is very probably a reference to the fact that in 29 BC Pergamum became the first city in Asia to build a temple dedicated to the imperial cult worship of the Roman emperor Augustus. Pergamum was also given the title 'Thrice Neokoros', because there were three temples dedicated to the Roman emperors, in which they were worshipped as gods. Although the Roman Empire promoted polytheism, under Domitian (AD 81–96), worship of the emperor was made mandatory and a test of one's loyalty to the state.

This is probably why Antipas is specifically honoured as someone who, like Stephen, was martyred there rather than renounce his faith. The Lord Jesus, however, rebukes the Christians in Pergamum

THE THEATRE, PERGAMUM

who had indeed compromised their faith under the pressure of paganism, as Balaam had done before (2 Peter 2:15–16).

The sword was a symbol of Roman rule, so Jesus reminds them that he alone possesses the true and ultimate authority, not Rome, symbolised by his 'sharp, double-edged sword' (Revelation 2:12). The meaning of the 'white stone' (Revelation 2:17) is not certain. It is possibly a reference to a 'pebble' or tessera, used in a law court to indicate the acquittal of the accused. The new name written on it gives us assurance of our forgiveness and acceptance by the Lord Jesus Christ.

The pressure to tolerate heresy and immorality under the guise of 'alternative lifestyles' and multi-faith worship is probably as strong now as it was in Pergamum. Our responsibility is to remain pure and faithful to God alone, then we will 'overcome'. Like the manna provided in the wilderness, as we seek his strength, Jesus provides us with 'hidden manna' to sustain us (Revelation 2:17). Pergamum reminds us that no power on earth can thwart God's purposes for us if we remain faithful to our calling.

THE STAR OF DAVID FROM THE RED BASILICA, PERGAMUM

Sardis

'To the angel of the church in Sardis write: These are the words of him who holds the seven spirits of God and the seven stars. I know your deeds; you have a reputation of being alive, but you are dead. Wake up! Strengthen what remains and is about to die, for I have not found your deeds complete in the sight of my God. Remember, therefore, what you have received and heard; obey it, and repent. But if you do not wake up, I will come like a thief, and you will not know at what time I will come to you. Yet you have a few people in Sardis who have not soiled their clothes. They will walk with me, dressed in white, for they are worthy.' (Revelation 3:1–4)

The city of Sardis was situated on the eastern bank of the Pactolus River at the southern end of the Hermus Valley, about eighty kilometres east of Smyrna and north-east of Ephesus.

The earliest settlement occupied the northern slopes of Mount Tmolus, its citadel situated on a high rocky spur, which was well fortified and easily defended. The Pactolus River, flowing at its base like a moat, ensured the city was virtually impregnable.

The wealth of Sardis was derived from gold found in the sandy shores of the Pactolus, from wool, the manufacture of textiles and jewellery. It is in Sardis that gold and silver coins were first minted by the opulent King Croesus. Due to its strategic location, as well as commercial importance on the East–West trade routes, Sardis became the capital of the ancient Lydian empire.

Ironically, because the citadel was built on such a steep, high hill, Croesus the last Lydian king, was complacent about its defence, convinced it did not need guarding. The city fell in 546 BC to Cyrus, the Persian ruler, after his soldiers observed how a Lydian descended the steep hill using steps cut into the rock to regain his lost helmet. Using this secret path the Persians entered the acropolis and captured Sardis. The people of Sardis failed to learn the lesson, because in 214 BC the city fell again, this time to Antiochus the Great who used the same tactics. Sardis is also remembered as the place from where Xerxes invaded Greece and Cyrus marched against his brother Artaxerxes.

THE SYNAGOGUE, SARDIS

THE TEMPLE OF ARTEMIS, SARDIS

In 334 BC, Alexander the Great captured Sardis but allowed it to remain independent. Just twelve years later, in 322 BC, it was taken by Antigonus. In 301 BC, the Seleucid kings, in turn, took the city and made it the home of their own governors. Sardis became independent again in 190 BC, as part of the Pergamum empire before eventually succumbing to Roman rule.

Sardis was also famous for its impressive Temple of Artemis as well as its mystery cults, especially one associated with Cybele. Built in the fourth century BC, the Temple of Artemis was 100 metres long and 50 metres wide, with 78 Ionic columns, each over 17 metres high. Some of these columns still remain standing today. There was also a large Jewish synagogue in Sardis, over 120 metres long and 18 metres wide. This was three times larger than any synagogue found in Palestine. An earthquake in AD 17 devastated the entire city. The emperor Tiberius gave Sardis a dispensation, freeing the city from taxation, and also helped to fund its restoration. Sardis never, however, regained its former glory.

In the first century, Sardis also had a large Christian community. It is the fifth church addressed by the Lord Jesus in the book of Revelation. The letter to 'the angel of the church in Sardis' (Revelation 3:1) suggests, however, that the church was infected with the same complacent attitude as the city. They were relying on their reputation, and failing to remain vigilant, as the city had twice failed before.

Jesus warns them, 'you have a reputation of being alive, but you are dead' (Revelation 3:1). His call to the Christians of Sardis, as to us in our day, is to 'Wake up! Strengthen what remains . . .' (Revelation 3:2). The reference to those 'dressed in white' (Revelation 3:5) would similarly have been familiar in a city renowned for its luxury clothing industry. The faithful who remain vigilant will indeed share in the triumphal coming of our Lord.

THE GYMNASIUM, SARDIS

Colosse

Paul, an apostle of Christ Jesus by the will of God, and Timothy our brother, To the holy and faithful brothers in Christ at Colosse: Grace and peace to you from God our Father. We always thank God, the Father of our Lord Jesus Christ, when we pray for you, because we have heard of your faith in Christ Jesus and of the love you have for all the saints – the faith and love that spring from the hope that is stored up for you in heaven and that you have already heard about in the word of truth, the gospel that has come to you. (Colossians 1:1–6)

Colosse

Colosse is situated on the great East–West trade route across Asia Minor where the roads from Sardis and Ephesus join, about twenty kilometres from Hierapolis and sixteen from Laodicea. The city was built over the Lycus River at the head of a gorge on one of the tributaries of the Maeander, about five kilometres from Mount Cadmus.

Two streams, one from the north and the other from the south pour into the Lycus and disappear under the city. The chalky deposits in the water have gradually formed a natural petrified arch, beneath which the current flows. This gave rise to superstitious beliefs about angelic appearances. For instance, they believed that the archangel Michael was their protecting saint.

Colosse was a prosperous mercantile city renowned for its wool and cloth-dyeing industries from as early as the fifth century BC during the time of the Lydian and Persian empires. Xerxes, for

THE CALCIUM TAVERTINES AT PAMUKKALE NEAR COLOSSE

instance, visited Colosse in 481 BC, and Cyrus the Younger in 401 BC. The city gave its name to 'collossinus', an unusual coloured wool, probably dyed dark red or purple. By the time Paul wrote his epistle to them, however, the city had declined in influence, eclipsed by its neighbouring cities (Colossians 4:13, 16). This was in part due to the re-routing further west of the road from Sardis to Pergamum to ensure it went via Laodicea instead.

Paul had spent three years in Ephesus in which, 'all the Jews and

Greeks who lived in the province of Asia heard the word of the Lord' (Acts 19:10). During this time Epaphras, Philemon, Onesimus, Archippus and Apphia, who were all from the region of Colosse, came to faith in Jesus Christ (Philemon 2:10, Colossians 4:9, 12). Epaphras returned to Colosse and helped found a church there (Colossians 1:7). He also ministered in the cities of Hierapolis and Laodicea (Colossians 2:1; 4:12–13). The church at Colosse met in the home of Philemon (Philemon 2). It is possible that Apphia and Archippus were his wife and son, and that Archippus was the pastor of the church (Colossians 4:17).

There was a significant Jewish presence in the area since Alexander the Great had settled Phrygia with Jews from Babylon. Cicero estimated that over 10,000 Jewish men alone lived in the Laodicea–Hierapolis–Colosse area. The distinctive features of religious life in Colosse included not only the local pagan worship of Cybele and superstitions concerning angels, but also a mixture of Jewish legalism, gnosticism and Eastern mysticism. It was this cocktail of error which Paul refuted in his letter to the young church there (Colossians 2:8–9, 16–23).

Paul uses the vocabulary of the gnostic heretics, such as 'fullness', 'wisdom', 'perfect' and 'complete' but invests them with Christian meaning to describe our relationship with Jesus Christ. The little word 'all' is used thirty times to stress the pre-eminent, universal and completed work of Jesus Christ (Colossians 1:15–18; 3:11). We therefore don't have to worry about angelic

HONAZ DAGI MOUNTAINS BEHIND COLOSSE

mediators or legalistic practices. Colosse reminds us not to let anyone 'deceive you by fine-sounding arguments' (Colossians 2:4), that 'no-one takes you captive through hollow and deceptive philosophy' (Colossians 2:8), or 'judge you by what you eat or drink' (Colossians 2:16). We are saved by grace alone through faith in Jesus Christ.

It was Paul's hope that he would visit Colosse after his anticipated release from prison in Rome (Philemon 22). It is not known whether he did so. Shortly after Paul wrote his letter, the towns of the Lycus Valley, including Colosse, were destroyed by a major earthquake in AD 61. Although rebuilt, Colosse gradually declined in influence, increasingly overshadowed by Laodicea and Hierapolis. The legacy of Colosse is therefore not its secret rituals or prized coloured wool but the good news that everyone who believes in Jesus Christ becomes part of his body, the church, of which he is the Head (Colossians 1:18).

LYCUS VALLEY TOWARDS COLOSSE

Ephesus

To the angel of the church in Ephesus write: These are the words of him who holds the seven stars in his right hand and walks among the seven golden lampstands: I know your deeds, your hard work and your perseverance. I know that you cannot tolerate wicked men, that you have tested those who claim to be apostles but are not, and have found them false. You have persevered and have endured hardships for my name, and have not grown weary. Yet I hold this against you: You have forsaken your first love.
(Revelation 2:1–4)

Ephesus is situated at the mouth of the Cayster River, opposite the island of Samos on the west coast of what is now Turkey, between Smyrna and Miletus. Ephesus commanded a strategic location at the end of the great caravan route from the Middle East. It was also the natural point of departure across the Aegean Sea for Rome and Corinth. Ephesus therefore became the largest and most important city in the Roman province of Asia, the bridgehead between East and West. At its height the population of Ephesus is estimated to have exceeded 300,000 people. Its theatre on

CELSUS LIBRARY, EPHESUS

the side of Mt Pion seated 24,000. An artificial harbour was constructed to enable large ships to sail down the river to the city. An impressive road, 11 metres wide and lined with columns, ran from the harbour to the city, itself surrounded by a 9-kilometre wall. Ephesus was rebuilt and relocated several times on the slopes of two hills, Pion and Coressos. During the first century the harbour was already silting up so that today Ephesus is now 10 kilometres inland. This may explain why Paul met the elders at the port of Miletus (Acts 20:15–16).

The site was associated with the veneration of a grotesque fertility mother goddess which predated Greek civilisation. The worship of Artemis, as she became known in Greek, and then Diana in Latin, was influential and prosperous but degrading. Her temple, rebuilt in 356 BC after a fire, was over 140 metres long and 75 metres wide. It was open to the sky with two rows of 127 columns 20 metres high. The temple was the largest building in the Greek empire and became one of the seven wonders of the world until it was destroyed by the Goths in AD 263. The Ephesians believed the image of Artemis had fallen from heaven which suggests the rock may have been a meteorite (Acts 19:35). Silver coins bearing the words *Diana Ephesia* found throughout Asia testify to the claim that she was indeed worshipped all over the known world (Acts 19:27). So wealthy was Ephesus, in 334 BC its inhabitants were able to decline the generous offer of Alexander the Great to rebuild the temple, if he might have his name inscribed in it. They insisted a god could not

ODEUM, EPHESUS

dedicate a temple to another god. Ephesus was also famous for its Ephesia grammata or 'Ephesian letters'. These were occult formulae written on scrolls and talismans. Furthermore, Ephesus became the centre for the imperial cult worship of the Roman emperors. With three separate temples, it qualified for the prestigious title 'neokoros' meaning 'temple warden' of the emperors, three times over.

There was also a large colony of Jews in Ephesus. Josephus, the Jewish historian, tells us that they enjoyed a privileged position, able to worship freely on the Sabbath without penalty. Paul visited Ephesus briefly, accompanied by Priscilla and Aquila who stayed on and discipled Apollos and a growing church (Acts 18:18–21). On Paul's third missionary journey he returned to Ephesus and made it his base for nearly three years (Acts 19:1–20:1). From here missionaries such as Epaphras were sent out taking the gospel to Colosse, Laodicea and other cities in the Lycus Valley (Colossians 1:6–7; 2:1). Luke could write confidently that, 'all the Jews and Greeks who lived in the province of Asia heard the word of the Lord' (Acts 19:10).

It was inevitable therefore that sooner or later there would be a confrontation between the apostles of Christ and the followers of Diana, especially those who profited from her veneration, such as the Guild of Silversmiths. As people came to faith in Jesus Christ they burnt their occult scrolls and destroyed their idols. They knew

KURETES STREET, WITH THE CELSUS LIBRARY AND THE TEMPLE OF HADRIAN

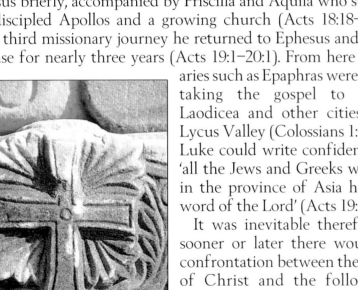

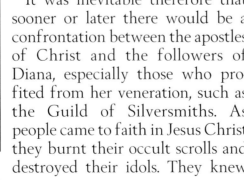

ST JOHN'S BASILICA, EPHESUS

they must make a clean break with paganism. It was a costly business. A drachma was a silver coin worth about a day's wage. Luke tells us that the value of the letters burnt came to 50,000 drachmas which would have been the annual income of 150 men (Acts 19:17–20).

Because the livelihood of the silversmiths was threatened, they incited the people against Paul (Acts 19:23–34). The crowd seized Paul's companions and stormed into the stadium where they shouted 'Great is Artemis of the Ephesians' for two whole hours before the city clerk could calm them down. Paul had to be restrained from appearing. The clerk warned the mob of the serious consequences of their riot which was illegal. In so doing Luke records the official Roman judgement that Paul and the other Christians were innocent of any crime against the State (Acts 19:35–41). It is possible that Paul had this mob violence in mind when he wrote later, 'I fought wild beasts in Ephesus' (1 Corinthians 15:32).

When Paul left Ephesus, Timothy stayed behind to pastor the congregation (1 Timothy 1:3). On his return to Jerusalem, Paul arranged to meet the elders of the church in Ephesus at Miletus. He charged them to be watchful shepherds of the flock of Christ predicting that 'savage wolves' would come, even from among their own, and would lead Christians astray (Acts 20:13–38).

The Apostle John subsequently ministered in Ephesus as well. The letters to the Seven Churches of the Apocalypse were written from Patmos, a small island about 80 kilometres south-west of Ephesus, on which John had probably been exiled for his faith (Revelation 1:9). As the largest city in proconsular Asia, Ephesus is the first of the seven churches addressed. The church is praised for its intolerance of false teachers, for its hard work and perseverance. But for all that, they are rebuked for losing their 'first love'. The Lord warns them not be proud but to remember their humble origins and repent (Revelation 2:1–7).

The great city of Ephesus including its church is long gone, its harbour silted up, its people driven away by malaria, its temples empty, the worship of Artemis now ancient history. It is a sober lesson. The abiding message of Ephesus is a loving warning to every 'successful' church. It is so easy to be busy serving Christ for the wrong reasons. When we lose sight of why Christ died for us, we can lose the thrill of knowing our sins are forgiven and fail to thank him as we once did. We must never forget, as John reminds us, 'we love because he first loved us' (1 John 4:19).

THE ROMAN THEATRE, EPHESUS

Athens

While Paul was waiting for them in Athens, he was greatly distressed to see that the city was full of idols. So he reasoned in the synagogue with the Jews and the God-fearing Greeks, as well as in the market-place day by day with those who happened to be there. A group of Epicurean and Stoic philosophers began to dispute with him. Some of them asked, 'What is this babbler trying to say?' Others remarked, 'He seems to be advocating foreign gods.' They said this because Paul was preaching the good news about Jesus and the resurrection. (Acts 17:16–18)

Athens was the ancient capital of the Greek province of Attica. Named after Athene, the goddess of wisdom, it was situated about 8 kilometres from the seaport of Piraeus on the Aegean Sea. Athens was connected to the port by a road between two long walls over 80 metres apart. Surrounded by the mountains of Parnis, Pentelicus, Hymettos and Aigaleon, the Athenian backdrop is often stark and barren.

Founded well before 1000 BC, Athens became the first city to experiment with democratic government. Destroyed by the Persians in the fifth century BC, Athens was rebuilt by Pericles on an impressive scale. Using tribute money from the Athenian empire, as well as from trade and commerce, beautiful buildings were erected which centred on the Acropolis, a 170-metre high focal point of the city. The Parthenon, for example, was dedicated to the goddess Athena and contained a spectacular frieze of a great procession containing four hundred people as well as two hundred animals. The Areopagus, named after Mars, the god of thunder, was situated on a spur on the western side of the Acropolis above the Agora or marketplace.

With a population of 250,000, Athens was the seat of Greek culture and learning, science and philosophy. The university became the most prestigious in the world with four great schools of philosophy – Platonic, Epicurean, Peripatetic and Stoic. It was the home of both

OLYMPIAN ZEUS, ATHENS

PARTHENON, ACROPOLIS, ATHENS

132

Aristotle and Plato, who founded his own Academy there in 388 BC. Socrates fared less well and was put to death in Athens in 399 BC. Even under Roman rule from 146 BC Athens continued to play an important role as the foremost university town of the empire, its influence reaching as far as Tarsus, Antioch and Alexandria.

Athens was also famous for its tolerance of religious belief, and was renowned for its temples, shrines, statues and monuments. Paul was deeply upset by this misguided religious zeal. The word Luke uses to describe the idols of Athens is found nowhere else in the Bible. It implies Athens was smothered or swamped by a forest of idols. Paul made one brief visit to Athens on his way from Macedonia to Corinth (1 Thessalonians 3:1). While there he seized the opportunity to teach and preach about Jesus Christ among the Jews in the local synagogue and also in the open air at the market place (Acts 17:17).

Areopagus is also the name of the venerable court which met to debate questions of religion and morality and authorise which teachers could lecture in public. Paul was therefore brought before the Areopagus to be examined regarding his teaching. So frequently did Paul speak of the resurrection of Jesus, they thought he was actually promoting two different gods, Jesus and Anastasis.

Despite their pantheon of gods, the Athenians had also built an altar 'to an unknown god' just in case they had missed one out. This Paul took as his starting point.

He began by identifying with them and emphasized what they could agree about God, quoting from their own poets. He stressed, however, that the one true God does not live in temples made by people, but created the whole world and revealed himself fully and finally in the Lord Jesus Christ (Acts 17:24–31). Although the Athenians did not believe in the resurrection or in a future judgement day, Paul refused to compromise his gospel and stressed both. He spoke of the facts of the resurrection of Jesus and

TOWER OF THE WINDS IN THE ROMAN FORUM, ATHENS

challenged his hearers to consider the implications for their own destiny. Our generation is very similar – dismissive of the supernatural claims of Jesus Christ yet incredibly superstitious and fascinated by the paranormal. While we must look for common ground in our evangelism we must not compromise the truth, and must make repentance and faith in Jesus Christ the issue.

It appears that only a handful of people came to believe as a result of Paul's initial ministry in Athens. However, Dionysius, a member of the Areopagus, is specifically mentioned as well as a woman named Damaris (17:34). We must not be surprised if many people will not believe our testimony either. By God's grace, some will, and in God's own good time, God will use them to lead others to himself also (2 Timothy 2:2). Our responsibility is to remain faithful to the gospel and, like Paul, God will make us fruitful.

Corinth

Paul left Athens, and went to Corinth. There he met a Jew named Aquila, a native of Pontus, who had recently come from Italy with his wife Priscilla, because Claudius had ordered all the Jews to leave Rome. Paul went to see them, and because he was a tentmaker as they were, he stayed and worked with them. Every Sabbath he reasoned in the synagogue, trying to persuade Jews and Greeks. (Acts 18:1–4)

Corinth is located at the western end of a narrow isthmus joining the southern Greek peninsula of Peloponnesus with the mainland to the north, about 70 kilometres from Athens. Situated at the foot of the Acrocorinth, a 566-metre hill towering over the plain below, and surrounded by a 10-kilometre wall, Corinth was easily defended and made a good fortress. The city was also blessed with two harbours, at Cenchreae, 14 kilometres to the east on the Saronic Gulf, and Lechaeum 2.5 kilometres to the west on the Corinthian Gulf.

TEMPLE OF APOLLO, CORINTH

The isthmus at Corinth was therefore a natural land bridge between the Ionian Sea and the Aegean Sea.

Given its strategic location, dominating the North–South road as well as the East–West shipping routes, Corinth was considered the key to Greece. According to Thucydides, the first ships of war were built at Corinth in 664 BC. As early as 850 BC, the Greek poet Homer also described Corinth as a 'wealthy' city. Indeed, from about 350 BC until 250 BC Corinth became the most influential and wealthiest city in Greece, rivalling even Athens. As part of the Achaean League, however, Corinth was eventually drawn into conflict with Rome and totally destroyed in 146 BC. The Roman consul Mummius burnt the city to the ground, killing all the men and forcing the women and children into slavery. It remained desolate for over a century.

In 44 BC Julius Caesar decided to rebuild the city as a Roman colony, re-populating it with both freed Italians as well as many slaves. It soon became a vital hub within the Roman Empire and capital of the new province of Achaia, ruled by its own proconsular governor. It is estimated that in the first century, the population included 250,000 freed persons and 400,000 slaves. The famous Isthmian games were held nearby every two years bringing sportsmen, gamblers, merchants and traders to the city from all over the Mediterranean.

The wealth of Corinth was derived largely from shipping and commerce since the ports of Lechaeum and Cenchreae were connected by an overland ship-road. The cargo from large ships was transported over the narrow peninsula while smaller ships were actually hauled overland from one port to the other by a series of rollers. This enabled ships to avoid the longer and more dangerous sea route to the south around Cape Malea which was liable to severe storms in winter (Acts 27:13–20).

Although now a Roman city, Corinthians continued to worship the pagan gods of Greece. Shrines have been discovered dedicated to

Apollo, Hermes, Athena and Poseidon, the sea god. It was also a major centre for healing with a temple of Asclepius and Hygieia. Corinth was renowned, however, for its temple dedicated to Venus or Aphrodite the goddess of love. The cult of Venus had been popular in Corinth long before the city's destruction by the Romans and was revived in the new city. The temple was situated on the top of the Acrocorinth. According to Strabo, the temple was popular with sailors and brought great wealth to the city, with, he claimed, over one thousand temple prostitutes.

In a prevailing culture where immorality was the accepted norm, Corinth was especially renowned for its licentiousness (1 Corinthians 5:1–5; 6:9–20). So much so that 'to Corinthianize' became a derogatory euphemism within Greek culture.

When Paul visited Corinth in 50 AD on his second missionary journey, it was a new and impressive but utterly depraved city. Near the centre of the city was a large marble-paved market with many shops known as the Agora. Paul mentions that the meat sold here had been dedicated to idols (1 Corinthians 8:1–13; 10:25). Nearby was the Bema, a large elevated platform with benches on three sides. It is probably here that Paul was brought before Gallio, the proconsul and brother of Seneca (Acts 18:12–18). In the residential area, archaeologists have also discovered a lintel inscribed 'Synagogue of the Hebrews' which may have been where Paul proclaimed the gospel and, when eventually rejected, founded a church next door at the home of Titius Justus (Acts 18:1–8).

Despite such a notorious reputation, where its people were poisoned by immorality and hardened by wealth and materialism, God nevertheless sent Paul, Aquila and his wife Priscilla, together with Silas, Timothy, Apollos and Titus to Corinth to preach the gospel. Paul stayed here for eighteen months and by God's grace many people were brought to faith in Jesus Christ. Paul wrote his

THE LECHAION WAY, CORINTH

letters to the church in Thessalonica as well as to Rome from Corinth and sent at least two letters back to them. The number of Latin names mentioned in Paul's letter to the Romans gives evidence of the fruitfulness of their labours there (Romans 16:21–27). These letters contain some of the most sobering as well as sublime teaching about love in the New Testament (Romans 1:18–32; 1 Corinthians 5:1–12 & 13:1–13). The controversies raised today about similar moral issues would suggest that perhaps our culture has more in common with Corinth than any other city in the New Testament. For that reason we too can take courage from the vision the Lord gave to Paul when he was tempted to give up on them, '*Do not be afraid; keep on speaking, do not be silent. For I am with you, and no-one is going to attack and harm you, because I have many people in this city*' (Acts 18:9–10).

137

THE TEMPLE
OF APOLLO,
CORINTH

139

Rome

And so we came to Rome. The brothers there had heard that we were coming, and they travelled as far as the Forum of Appius and the Three Taverns to meet us. At the sight of these men Paul thanked God and was encouraged. When we got to Rome, Paul was allowed to live by himself, with a soldier to guard him. (Acts 28:14–16)

Rome was the most famous city of the ancient world, synonymous with both power and empire. Situated on the Tiber River, about 30 kilometres from the Mediterranean Sea, the first settlement was on the Palatine Hill and has been dated from 753 BC. The city gradually expanded to cover the seven surrounding hills. Rome began as a monarchy ruled by kings from 753–510 BC. It then became a Republic until 31 BC when Caesar Augustus was appointed the first emperor of the Roman Empire.

In the first century AD, Rome

ROMAN FORUM, ROME

was the largest city in the world with a population exceeding one million, most of whom were slaves or plebeians. Roman citizens enjoyed 159 holidays a year, 93 of which were dedicated to sport, chariot races, games and performances sponsored by the government. The Circus Maximus, for example, could seat 200,000 people. At its height Rome contained 254 mills, 190 grain silos, 8 bridges, 8 great squares, 11 forums, 36 triumphal arches, 1,152 fountains, 28 public libraries, 2 circuses, 2 amphitheatres, 3 theatres, 11 hot spring baths and 865 private bath houses. About an eighth of the city was also laid out as beautiful parks and gardens.

Religion in Rome was essentially polytheistic. Augustus, for example, restored 82 temples in the city. Besides the traditional gods of Rome, the emperor became the focus of the empire, regarded as semi-divine while alive and achieving the status of god when dead. The imposition of the Imperial cult, the worship of the emperor, became a test of loyalty to the empire. It was because Jews and Christians refused to worship the emperor, as at Pergamum, that they came to be seen as a threat to the State (Revelation 2:13).

Priscilla and Aquila, who became co-workers with Paul in Corinth, were among the Jews expelled from Rome by the emperor Claudius in AD 49. This indicates that by this time, there was already a church in the capital although the Roman authorities did not yet appear to distinguish between Christians and Jews (Acts 18:2).

In Paul's letter to the church in Rome, written about AD 57, he expressed his desire to visit them on one of his missionary journeys, perhaps on route to Spain (Romans 15:24). Paul did indeed visit Rome three years later, but as a prisoner. He had appealed to Caesar during his trial before Festus the Roman Governor of Judea at Caesarea. Paul had been born a Roman citizen and therefore had the right to have his case heard by the emperor in Rome (Acts 22:28). Paul was confident that he and the Christian community would be vindicated from all

charges brought by the Jewish authorities (Acts 25). When Paul landed at Puteoli, believers from Rome travelled as far as the Forum of Appius, about 70 kilometres from Rome, to welcome him. Others met them at the Three Taverns, about 55 kilometres away, to escort Paul the remainder of the journey (Acts 28:13–15).

The book of Acts closes, confidently, with Paul in Rome, renting his own living quarters with a soldier to guard him. For two years he awaited his trial, free to receive visitors and proclaim, unhindered, the good news of the gospel at the heart of the Roman Empire (Acts 28:16–31). In his letter to the Philippians, probably written from Rome around AD 61, Paul gave some indication of the fruitfulness of his ministry, 'All the saints send you greetings, especially those who belong to Caesar's household' (Philippians 4:22).

In his last epistle, probably written from the notorious Marmertine Prison, Paul describes his trial. He foresees his impending death yet remains unshaken in his faith in God's sovereign purposes: 'At my first defence, no-one came to my support, but everyone deserted me. May it not be held against them. But the Lord stood at my side and gave me strength, so that through me the message might be fully proclaimed and all the Gentiles might hear it. And I was delivered from the lion's mouth. The Lord will rescue me from every evil attack and will bring me safely to his heavenly kingdom. To him be glory for ever and ever. Amen.' (2 Timothy 4:16–18)

Both Peter and Paul were among the many Christians, mostly unknown, martyred in Rome over the next 250 years before the eventual conversion of the Roman Empire under Constantine. Jesus had taught that the best way to defeat an enemy is to turn him into a friend. Paul himself had initially been an enemy of Christ and became his friend (Romans 5:10; Colossians 1:21–22). Through Paul and the small groups of believers persecuted and scattered across the vast Roman Empire, the Lord Jesus transformed the entire world. The blood of the martyrs was indeed the seed of the church.

THE COLOSSEUM, ROME

143

Further Reading & Useful Addresses

1. THE HISTORY AND ARCHAEOLOGY OF THE BIBLE LANDS

F. F. Bruce, *Jesus and Paul: Places They Knew* (London: Scripture Union)

Werner Keller, *The Bible as History, Illustrated Edition* (Oxford: Lion Publishing).

Alan Millard, *A Treasury of Bible Pictures* (Oxford: Lion)

David Rohl, *The Test of Time* (Century, London)

Derek Williams, *The Bible Chronicle* (Guildford, Eagle)

2. THE BEST GUIDEBOOKS TO THE BIBLE LANDS

Rosie Ayliffe, *The Rough Guide to Turkey* (Rough Guides)

Baedeker, *Baedeker's Turkey* (Fodors Travel Publications)

Beni Bown, *Eyewitness Travel: Greece* (Dorling Kindersley)

Beni Bown, *Eyewitness Travel: Guide: Italy* (Dorling Kindersley)

Tom Brosnahan & Pat Yale, *Lonely Planet: Turkey* (Lonely Planet)

Ronald Brownrigg, *Come See The Place* (London: Hodder and Stoughton)

Dorling Kindersley, *Dorling Kindersley Travel Guide to Jerusalem and the Holy Land* (Dorling Kindersley)

Dorling Kindersley, *Eyewitness Travel Guide: Rome* (Dorling Kindersley)

Fodor, *Fodor's Greece* (Fodors Travel Publications)

Helen Gillman, et al., *Lonely Plant: Italy* (Lonely Planet)

Andrew Humphreys, *Lonely Planet Guide: Israel and the Palestinian Territories* (Lonely Planet)

Madeline Reincke, *Baedeker's Rome* (Fodors Travel Publications)

Rough Guide, *The Rough Guide to Italy* (Rough Guides)

Rough Guide, *The Rough Guide to Israel and the Palestinian Territories* (Rough Guides)

Damien Simonis & Hugh Finlay, *Lonely Planet Jordan and Syria* (Lonely Planet)

Norman Wareham and Jill Gill, *Every Pilgrim's Guide to the Holy Land* (Norwich: Canterbury Press)

David Willett, et. al., *Lonely Planet: Greece* (Lonely Planet)

3. THE CONTEMPORARY SITUATION IN THE HOLY LAND

Gary Burge, *Whose Land? Whose Promise?* (Carlisle, Paternoster)

Colin Chapman, *Whose Promised Land?* (Oxford: Lion)

Kenneth Cragg, *Palestine: The Prize and Price of Zion.* (London: Cassell)

Salim Munyer, *Seeking & Pursuing Peace* (Jerusalem: Musalaha)

Michael Prior (ed), *They Came and They Saw, Western Experiences of the Holy Land* (London, Melisende)

4. THE LOCAL CHRISTIAN COMMUNITIES

Riah Abu El Assal, *Caught in Between* (London: SPCK)

Elias Chacour, *We Belong to the Land* (London, Marshall Pickering)

Kenneth Cragg, *The Arab Christian: A History in the Middle East* (London: Cassell)

William Dalrymple, *From the Holy Mountain* (London: Harper Collins)

Garth Hewitt, *Pilgrims and Peacemakers* (Oxford: Bible Reading Fellowship)

Garth Hewitt, *Candle of Hope* (Oxford: Bible Reading Fellowship)

Alison Hilliard & Betty Jane Bailey, *Living Stones Pilgrimage with the Christians of the Holy Land: A Guide* (London, Cassell)

Donald Wagner, *Dying in the Land of Promise* (London, Melisende)

5. Useful Christian Contacts in and for the Bible Lands

Amos Trust All Hallows on the Wall, 83 London Wall, London EC2M 5NA
Tel: 020-7588-2661. Fax: 020-7588-2663. e-mail info@amostrust.org
www.amostrust.org/index.html

The Alternative Tourism Group (ATG) PO Box 173, Beit Sahour, West Bank. via Israel. Tel: 972-2-6472151. Fax: 972-2-6472211.
e-mail: atg@p-ol.com

Bethlehem Bible College Hebron Road, PO Box 127, Bethlehem, West Bank, via Israel. Tel: 972-2-741190. Fax: 972-2-743278 email: bethbc@planet.edu www.bethlehembiblecollege.edu/

Bible Lands Society PO Box 50, High Wycombe, Buckinghamshire. HP15 7QU
Tel: 01494 521351 www.biblelands.co.uk

Christian Aid 35 Lower Marsh, Waterloo, London, SE1 7RL,
Tel: (+44) 020 7620 4444, email: info@christian-aid.org
www.christian-aid.org.uk

Churches Ministry Among Jewish People (CMJ), PO Box 14037, Jaffa Gate, Old City, Jerusalem. Tel: 972-2-627 7727.
Fax: 972-2-627 7730. e-mail: christch@netvision.net.il
www.cmj.org.uk/

Ecumenical Travel Service – The Middle East Council of Churches. Liaison Office, PO Box 14634, East Jerusalem 91146. via Israel. Tel: 972-2-6284493. Fax: 972-2-6284730

Evangelicals For Middle East Understanding (EMEU) PO Box 553 – Union, WA 98592-0553 USA. Tel: (404) 842-2578 email: MarilynBorst@aol.com www.emeu.net/index.html

The Intercontinental Church Society (ICS), 1 Athena Drive, Tachbook Park, Warwick, CV34 6NL www.ics-uk.org/

Living Stones c/o St Mary's University College, Strawberry Hill, Twickenham, TW1 4SX

The Middle East Council of Churches (MECC) PO Box 4259, Limassol, Cyprus.
Tel: +357 (5) 326 022 www.mecchurches.org

Sabeel Liberation Theology Centre PO Box 1248, Jerusalem.
Tel: 972-2-289415. Fax: 972-2-283869. e-mail: sabeel@plant.edu
www.sabeel.org/

St George's Cathedral St George's Cathedral Close, PO Box 19018, East Jerusalem 91190. via Israel. Tel: 972-2-283261. Fax: 972-2-273401
email: devedjer@netvision.net.il

The Garden Tomb Association PO Box 19462, Nablus Road, East Jerusalem, 91193. Tel: 972-2-272745 www.gardentomb.com/

World Vision PO Box 51399. An-Nuzha Building. 2 Abu Obeida Street, East Jerusalem. via Israel. Tel: 972-2-281793. Fax: 972-2-272065. www.worldvision.org/worldvision/master.nsf/home

For further articles on Israel–Palestine and the indigenous Christian community of the Holy Land see: www.sizers.org or email Stephen Sizer at stephen@sizers.org

For further information on the photographs, visit the website of Jon Arnold at www.jonarnold.com